"Paul writes a cand............ .....ding book on what it actually feels like to plant a church – all the highs and lows. Wise, vulnerable and immensely encouraging!" – **John Valentine, Dean of the Local Ministry Programme in the Diocese of Guildford**

"I am so glad that Paul Pavlou has written a book to share the valuable lessons he learnt from sharing the love of Jesus through church planting." – **Rev. Archie Coates, Vicar of Holy Trinity Brompton**

"Church planting is exciting, challenging and often exhausting but also extraordinarily effective in building up faith and growing the Church. I am so glad Paul Pavlou has written this book to take us through his own fascinating journey." – **Rev. Sarah Jackson, CEO of Revitalise Trust**

"An honest story of learning to obey the prompting of the Spirit from someone with a deep love for Jesus, for those who don't yet know Him, and a longing for the church to be all that God intended it to be... everywhere!" – **John Coles, former National Leader of New Wine**

JOURNAL OF A
CHURCH
PLANTER

A Window into the Life

Thank you to CCX for the encouragement, patience and hard work invested in helping me to make this possible. Thank you to St. Barnabas Church (North Finchley) for being so formative in my discipleship over the years, and for introducing me to Hayley. Thank you to our friends and family who have held us in prayer & for championing us throughout our marriage. Most of all, thank you Hayley, Evangeline and Zachary – I wouldn't want to do this with anyone else!

Foreword

I believe in church planting. I also believe that we are in a missionary situation in this country. Church planting is bucking the trend of declining numbers in institutional churches. It is extending the Kingdom of God. Church plants of different sizes and shapes are reaching new people in new and renewed ways. It is so exciting to see God working in this way and that is one reason why I have dedicated the last twenty-five years to planting churches and helping others to do so.

Peter Wagner, an American missionary, writer and teacher, wrote in a study for the Fuller Seminary in 1990 that 'planting new churches is the most effective evangelistic methodology known under heaven.' I believe this is still true today; that we are called to reach new people in new places with the Gospel of Jesus Christ and that church planting is going to be a part of that story.

Planting a church is an amazing, exciting adventure of faith. It is also filled with challenges and uncertainties. In this book, Paul Pavlou gives a stirringly honest, impassioned insight into the highs and lows of what we can experience when stepping out to answer God's call to plant a church. He has recorded with beautiful vulnerability his experiences of the highs and lows and charts a valuable path for others looking to do the same.

This book will be of huge value to anyone with a vision to plant a church. Paul offers personal reflections and advice on planting churches: how to scout out a location for a plant; how to build the right scaffolding for a plant with good foundations and relationships; honest reflections on some of the personal challenges and how to overcome them; joyful accounts of the good aspects, the moments of glimpsing the sunrise and excerpts from his journal. If you are thinking about or planning to plant a church, this book can be a companion for your journey, offering you encouragement and acknowledgement along the way.

I'm hugely grateful to leaders like Paul for how he has answered God's call, and I pray that this book will encourage those who are discerning if God is calling them to reach new people with the Gospel by planting a church.

The Rt. Rev. Dr. Ric Thorpe
The Bishop of Islington

Contents

Introduction: Setting the Scene; A Bit About Me and What I'm Sharing

Chapter 1: Scouting; A Prologue to Planting Preparation

Chapter 2: Scaffold; Forming Foundations and Connections

Chapter 3: Shaping; Allowing God to Shape the Church and Me

Chapter 4: Shadows; Shining a Light on the Shadow Side of Planting

Chapter 5: Sunrise; Light Overcomes the Darkness

Chapter 6: Snippets; Raw Diary Entries Over the Last Year

Conclusion: Summing up; I Don't Know How This Will All Pan Out, And That's OK!

About the Author

PAUL PAVLOU

Introduction: Setting the Scene; A Bit About Me and What I'm Sharing

The majority of what you are about to read was formed out of my journaling in the run up to church planting and in the first few months of it. Most of this was written live in the moment, with some retrospective insight and reflection woven through. At the time of publishing, I will be coming towards the end of my third academic year here; much has happened between my first ever journal entry and now. It's been an incredible ride and this book is a snapshot into the earliest days of it, as I think these are very formative for prospective church planters – hence wanting to share 'how it feels' in that chapter of the leader's life. Plenty more has been learnt since the bulk of this writing and there's lots I would do differently if I were to start again. Whilst this isn't the space for unpacking that, I will share the headline, which is 'do the prep work, take it slow – go gently, and enjoy the small wins along the way.' The story isn't finished here: it will continue long after we move on. I'm so grateful for all the highs and lows we've experienced along the way. It has been a privilege to be part of what God has been doing and I can't wait to see what He will continue to do in the future.

At the back of this book you'll find two QR codes. One will take you to the 'Journal of a Church Planter' video series, where each episode is an interview matching each chapter of the book. The other code will take you to my 'Church Plant Chat' podcast which is a podcast of interviews with a range of UK based church planters sharing their wisdom on church planting. Both of these resources are free for you to access and use as you wish.

In the run up to planting and now having come close to getting through my twelve to eighteen months of it, I have been repeatedly asked the question 'Why church planting?' The long answer is that seeing planting happen has always been normal for me. Growing up as a teenager, I witnessed my dad getting sent out to plant a church into what was a closed down building. I wasn't walking with God at the time, but even then, I could see there was something special in what my dad and his team were embarking on.

Seeing my dad do that within the Church of England (CofE), I had assumed that planting is just what we do – that planting is normal. I have since learnt that, within the CofE at least, this is not the case, which is puzzling to me as so much of it seems to be so like the core elements of ordinary parish ministry and the church of the New Testament.

Due to my own experience of failed planting plans over the years, the realisation of how hard it is, and the clear need for more churches and leaders in the country, it has become a growing passion and longing of mine to see that church planting becomes normal across all denominations. Because every church that has ever existed is a church plant, it's just that over time some people have forgotten that.

Over the years, I began to develop a sense of call to preaching and then leadership, and so I eventually pushed the door to pursue Ordination training. Whilst at Theological college, the call to church planting/ revitalisation began to grow and crystallise. I hadn't gone into theological college thinking that I was going to be a church planter; I was very for it and believed in it but didn't necessarily think that would be my trajectory. Yet it formed into that nonetheless and so for my curacy I was seeking out a church planting curacy, which I thought I had found. However, after three years of trying to get permission to start a church plant, we were unsuccessful (this will be unpacked further in the 'Scouting' section to follow). What I have realised all throughout this process, is that at every step of the way, none of it has been what I originally anticipated it being. At every turn things have changed, and God hasn't stuck to my plans. This run up to planting and my first year of doing it, really, has been an ongoing process of me repeatedly having to get to a place of contentment and excitement, even despite it time and time again not being what I'd thought... and that's OK!

With that in mind, the following write ups are a compilation of diary entries, expanded thoughts, self-reflection and journeying in the run up to my experience of church planting and the first fifteen months (or so) of it. There are not many references to other people or my wonderful team because this is mostly a window into what's going on in the head and heart of someone going through the planting process, so it may come across as a bit "me focused" at times, but the idea is to let you into my world as a church planter – or at least for you to see a snapshot of it. This book is not necessarily about all the individual conversations, cultural settings, change management, team building etc. that comes with a church graft-plant like ours. Rather, it's an inner monologue of experiences faced whilst doing all that 'stuff'. This is a glorified journal of a church planter in the thick of my early days in the role; a window into this life. That will mean that the church planting story will obviously be unfinished and so will my development and growth as a leader within it, because it's only an account of the early days – but that's the point!

I want this to be as real-time a reflection of what it's like trying to plant in the first place and then actually give insight into what it can feel like in the first year or so – both the good and the challenging, without the knowledge that it will all end well. Instead, I'd like to share this with you (especially emerging planters) with the understanding that I just don't know how it will all pan out. On multiple occasions throughout a week, in one day even, this thing often feels like it's all hanging on a knife-edge. Each step can feel like it's faced with a contradictory combination of uncertainty and confidence. Facing fear of the unknown is at constant tension with joyful highs of seeing God at work. Learning to stay balanced and hold your nerve whilst walking this knife-edge feels like a large portion of this lifestyle at times.

Obviously, I can't share everything I have experienced, but I have tried to be as open and vulnerable as I think I can publicly, whilst trying to honour those I have encountered along the way. What you will soon see as you read, is that most of the struggles are really with myself rather than with people. There have been tricky conversations along the way and plenty of institutional frustrations, but really, the spotlight of the battles has primarily been down to my own issues, brokenness, and need for growth as a leader — as a follower of Jesus (which church planting seems to have brought to the surface and has forced me to face and learn from).

It's my hope that what I share will encourage emergent and early day planters (and maybe even some who are preparing for ministry in general), letting them know that others have gone before them and may have gone through similar highs and lows. I aim to let them know that we don't have to be superhuman; that it's OK if it's not all shiny social media posts; that it's alright if it turns out different to what you thought and that ultimately, we can rely on God's faithfulness and in return try our best to be faithful in this work.

By giving the back story and unpacking my spiritual/emotional/mental and practical experience of these early days, it's also my hope that those reading will feel like they are engaging in a shared experience and they themselves might be able to connect with others on their journey too. You are not alone in this!

What you encounter along the way in your own planting story may not be what you thought, but know that that's OK. God's got you, and the Church!

Chapter 1
Scouting; A Prologue to Planting Preparation

Proverbs 3:5-6
'Trust in the Lord with all your heart
and lean not on your own understanding;
in all your ways submit to Him,
and He will make your paths straight.'

Stumbling and Scouting

Over the three years of my Curacy, my wife and I had been scouting out an area to plant a church.

All in all (including two smaller conversations that never got further than an initial conversation) we have had five false starts, and no church had been planted. We definitely stumbled our way through!

After the final attempt fell through, we prayerfully and painfully drew a line under planting in that area. This was not only painful for us, but also for my training incumbent and our church, as he and they were all invested in this thing – they were so for us. I felt awful for letting people down, having had conversations about people coming with us to plant and sharing dreams with each other about how that could happen. We had all invested in each other and then it just ended, and it hurt. Even as I write this, I feel the pain of that loss. Church planting, even in its failure, has a profound ripple effect. We had five failed attempts. That means in theory that five churches could have been planted, and none of them were. My heart races now just as much as it did back then when I reflect on this, because whilst I made my fair share of mistakes in trying to get these off the ground, there is also a lack of continuity and vision in how we in the CofE enable planting to happen with the freedom it needed to do so. We cannot shy away from this or pretend like it's not an issue, because it is. I've experienced it and it's not OK – we can do better.

Having no options left to plant and drawing a line under our planting journey in Curacy, I took some time to reflect on each of these failed attempts. As I did so, I realised that I had walked or rather stumbled my way through a specific pattern with each round of 'scouting' that took place.

Though I had nothing to show for my attempts to plant a church, I found contentment in the process that I had been subconsciously working through. It turned out to be a robust pattern, which encouraged me with the peace of knowing that my wife and I had been faithful to God's call throughout our 'scouting' phase. If nothing else, this scouting pattern had helped us to work through and discern that that area was not in fact where God wanted us to plant, but rather may have helped pave the way for someone else in the future.

We were prepared to share the Gospel, but Jesus simply did not open the doors for us there. Through the working out of the stages below, we were able to find peace in God's will and get back up again in the confidence that He had something else in mind – we just needed to scout out where!

Before looking at the pattern, I think it's worth getting our posture right. One of the things I've learnt when discerning where to plant/revitalise a church is that our hearts and heads need to be postured correctly before the Lord, and respectfully before those who have gone before us in the land we are seeking to walk into. In 1 Chronicles 13–14 we read about David moving the ark as well as triumphing over the Philistines.[1]

There are three takeaways from these chapters which I think we can apply to our discerning of where to plant churches. The first is in 1 Chronicles 13:1 – it's here that David 'conferred with each of his officers, the commanders of thousands and commanders of hundreds.' David communicated with his team; he worked this decision through with them. He did not charge off as a lone ranger and isolated, but shared his thoughts with others, letting them in on the plan.

---

[1] 'Bible in One Year', p453, Nicky Gumbel. I am typing this chapter up approximately ten months since I originally wrote it in my notepad. I think I was reading the Bible in One Year at the time, and I cannot for the life of me remember if this thought process about David in 1 Chronicles (and as a result the application to church planting) came naturally to me or if it was inspired by Nicky Gumbel's commentary. So, to make sure I've got the basis covered I have footnoted the page of the commentary where Gumbel speaks about David.

It is very easy for wires to get crossed with church planting, especially at the early stages of discernment, so I think it's worth making every effort to meet and talk to people about what God may be calling us into on that 'patch.' Even if you don't see eye to eye with them or they are not keen on your arrival, at least you've been courteous and included them within the process. I certainly could have done more of this in my first experiences of trying to get a plant off the ground – I often wonder if they would have been more fruitful if I had.

The second take away from David's story is in 1 Chronicles 13:12–14: '12 David was afraid of God that day and asked, "How can I ever bring the ark of God to me?" 13 He did not take the ark to be with him in the City of David. Instead, he took it to the house of Obed-Edom the Gittite.14 The ark of God remained with the family of Obed-Edom in his house for three months, and the Lord blessed his household and everything he had.' By God's presence simply being in Obed-Edom's house, he was in turn blessed by God. I can say with embarrassment that so often in the discernment stage and later too, that I all too often go into pragmatic mode to get things done, rather than simply taking the time to be still and acknowledge God's presence in the space that I'm in or looking to step into. I have caught myself far too many times trying to run ahead of God's presence when 'discerning' where to plant or plan how that looks now that I'm in the job, or, trying to do things in my own strength or forgetting that without His presence that this is all in vain; trying to accomplish, rather than acknowledge God's goodness in a place and my life. Not only that, but at times there has been a very definite pride in my heart where I've thought that I need to be the one to bring God's presence somewhere because it's not there already. I cringe even whilst writing and re-reading that sentence. If nothing else, this planting journey is revealing to me my distinct lack of humility. Anyway, God is good, and He forgives, phew!

I came across this short yet profound prayer recently that I think would be a good way to round off this second point: 'May I have vision and courage to join God in the places He's already working rather than feel responsible for bringing Him with me.'[2]

Thirdly, and very much linked to God's presence going before us and blessing us, is David asking God's permission before making plans and moving forward. In 1 Chronicles 14:8–17, twice David inquired of God about what he should do. David sought God's instruction and permission before moving ahead with his plans. When we are discerning where to plant/revitalise a church, even if the options in front of us seem obvious, we need to properly inquire of God to show us the way. Isaiah 55:8–9, '"For My thoughts are not your thoughts, neither are your ways My ways," declares the Lord. "As the heavens are higher than the earth, so are My ways higher than your ways and My thoughts than your thoughts."'

---

[2] Prayer: Forty days of practice', Prayer 3, Justin McRoberts & Scott Erickson

His ways are not our ways, and so even if something seems plain enough and humanly perceivable and plannable, it does not mean it's God's will. I think it's all too easy for us to get on our high horse about being ground-breaking pioneers who are going to shake things up and bring Kingdom change and therefore we pray prayers that are more of a list of demands for what we want God to do – essentially testing God, trying to bend His will to ours because we think we are on some sort of mission. When really, we should be humbling ourselves before the presence of God and reverently inquiring of Him to show us the way. Michael Mayne, in his book called 'Prayer', cites Max Warren who says this: 'Our first task in approaching another person, another culture, another religion, is to take off our shoes, for the place we are approaching is holy. Else we may find ourselves treading on men's dreams. More seriously still, we may forget that God was here before our arrival.'[3] I don't know if this quote was in reference to church planting/revitalisation, but this is the lens I read it with.

When we are setting out to do this thing, we need to be speaking with others along the way, acknowledging God's presence seriously during it all, and reverently seek His permission as we step out. The moment we fail to do this, we trip up on our own pride and sense of misplaced mission; we forget that God has already been at work with these people we are trying to reach/disciple; we do more harm than

---

[3] Max Warren, cited in 'Prayer' by Michael Mayne, p39.

good in trampling all over those who we think are just getting in our way – forgetting that the ground is holy, because it's all God's anyway.

I think the posture developed by these three things of communication, presence and permission will give us a much better chance of discerning with humility as we search out where God is calling us to. Hopefully, the pattern I have unpacked here helps to ensure that we keep this posture along the way, or at least can remind us to refocus our intentions as we go.

Scouting Pattern Summary

This scouting pattern involves four stages:

seek - step - sow - surrender

(with purposeful 'space' plotted throughout the pattern).

With each scouting phase I underwent, I found it important to:

'Seek' the Lord's will;
'Step' out in faith to give it a go;
'Sow' into it – investing time, emotion, prayer, energy, meetings, planning;
'Surrender' the whole process to God and His will each time; and
Give 'Space' for the Spirit to move or to catch our breath, allow headspace and remain creative.

It's not a particularly fancy or complicated process, but when you are 'all in' committed to each stage of it, I soon found that the task of scouting out an area to plant in the fullest sense (with all the Deanery/ Diocesan conversations and such like included) can be an incredibly draining one spiritually, emotionally, mentally and physically.

In fact, I would highly recommend hand picking just a couple of close friends to embark on this process with you so that you are supported and upheld throughout, as it can leave you catching your breath at times. For me, I had my Training Incumbent helping and holding me through each attempt. He and his wife were absolute life savers, and they felt the pain my wife and I felt with each disappointment. I'm so grateful to them for caring for us as they did throughout the journey. I don't think I would have continued pursuing church planting if it were not for their support. Make sure you journey with someone mature in the faith as you scout and discern where to land. Remember, this isn't even the church planting bit, it's not even the preparing to plant bit – it's just the prologue!

Practising the Pattern

So, what could each of these stages look like in the day to day of this scouting pattern?

Seek

- Essentially, the bulk of 'seek' is prayer.

- Prayer walk the area you're scouting.

- Pray with friends about it.

- Take a note from David's book and seek God's permission before making any sort of plans to do things (1 Chronicles 14:9-16).

- Pray, but also wait on the Lord, not rushing into the 'steps' and just allowing for a prayerful pause before embarking any further.

- We also need to seek out our emotions. What are the things we are passionate about? Who are the people that we find ourselves praying and interceding for?

- This stage is also good for asking yourself, 'Why plant here?' or, 'Why plant at all?'

- Our egos and motivations need to be kept in check at every stage of the scouting. The heart can be deceitful, and our eyes can be greedy. I cannot stress enough how important it is to seek God's help in humility. Whilst there were many frustrations and barriers to us being able to plant, I don't doubt for a moment that my own pride and ego got in the way too! I'm constantly amazed at my lack of humility and holiness, hence the need to keep seeking the Lord repeatedly.

Step

- This is taking the faith and confidence built up during the 'seek' stage in times of prayer, worship and waiting on the Lord and using it to take a step forward and commit to being 'all in' with this church plant option.

- We need to hold prospective plant options lightly, yes, but I also think we need to be fully committed to the process and make ourselves vulnerable to it, despite possible disappointments we may face. God will give us all we need in those moments of disappointment and the Spirit will give us the strength to get up again when we are knocked down – so go for it. Step out in the knowledge that Jesus walks with you and has your back whatever the outcome.

Sow

- This is the process of taking our prayers and steps into a variety of actions and investments into the prospective project. This can involve (but is by no means limited to) the following:

    o Conversations with:

        ◆ A whole range of people in your current church, including PCC.

        ◆ People from the church you may be grafting into i.e. if it isn't a blank canvas plant and you're revitalising a church, then you really need to talk to that remnant thoroughly before committing to going in with a team (see footnotes for some elaboration on this).[4] Essentially, your conversations and starting points will look different depending on the type of plant project you are called to.

♦ Those in the deanery (clergy, other church members, area dean).

---

[4] You won't need to go through the process of change management needed in a graft situation (at least not to begin with), so there's less people to talk to in that respect, simply because those people aren't there because it's quite literally 'blank.' However, you do want to ask questions and build relationships with prior clergy and pastors in the area you're planting into. They likely would have been serving there faithfully for years and will have a lot of wisdom to share. In the church graft situation, you're more likely to start the questions from within the church, because there's a small group of people already there to bring along the planting journey with you. But for the blank canvas you might want to think about going to the surrounding community to begin with and take an interest in what their needs and hopes are for the community and how a church could potentially benefit/serve them. I'd also be interested to ask clergy around the area/parish what they feel the Spirit has been doing there over the last few years, and learning from them what they feel have been the main Spiritual battle stories of the area and where they feel a lot of their intercessions have landed for those they are trying to reach. I.e., what is being contended for in prayer in that area that a blank canvas plant could potentially prioritise its prayer and mission around? Such questions are important to help one think about the process of planting, and others far more experienced than me will have lots of advice on this. The main point, however, is that the types of questions you ask and who you are asking will be different depending on the type of plant project, and even more important than that, to encourage you to have the confidence to ask the hard questions and to keep asking them until you have the clarity and peace you need before deciding if this is the right plant option for you. You can't go into either type of planting options without being 'all in' – clarity over some of these harder conversations will help you invest more fully.

- ◆ Whoever your denominational hierarchy is, i.e. archdeacons, bishops etc.

- o Writing up strategic documents, vision plans, looking at maps and researching the area, its demographics, church attendance, other churches nearby and so on.

- o Thinking through what shape the church plant may take depending on the context and make-up of the area; what/if any buildings are available; if it would be a plant from scratch or a graft, a fresh expression model etc.

Depending on the planting scenario you're looking at, conversations will vary and different sets of questions will need to be asked – much of which will need to be contextual to each plant option. For instance, the questions I would ask around a blank canvas church plant vs. a church plant graft would be very different. With a church graft plant set up, I would want to ask questions which give absolute clarity over what has been explained to the church remnant I would be inheriting (and planting a new congregation/team into). This is key. It's imperative that the congregation receiving the plant graft know the key changes that are coming their way ahead of the new plant team coming in, and that they have already taken significant steps towards embracing this. Otherwise, the church plant team and their leader going in will be facing a context filled with confusion and conflict over what should and should not be happening – this delays the mission and disrupts the relationship from the start. This is unfair for both groups of people: those receiving the plant team and those going into the project.

Quiz anyone involved at every level – from those high up in the Diocese right down to the members of the church you're going into. I would even go so far as to encourage some sort of covenantal agreement to be drawn up, agreed, and signed by all involved ahead of the plant team coming in, so as to make sure that everyone is on the same page and willing to drive forward with the work needed to be done. If you as the prospective planter do not feel at peace at the end of that process of questioning, then I would strongly advise you consider whether the option you're looking at is ready to have a plant team go in. Going into a church plant-graft is hard enough as it is without having to work from a minus point. Do the homework and ask the hard questions.

For a blank canvas church plant, the line of questioning is different as you have a different starting point and more flexibility.

Surrender

- This is arguably the most important of the four stages, although each is incredibly valuable. This was the one that kept knocking me for six in how hard it was to do, but also how incredibly freeing it was each time I was able to simply surrender the plans to God.

- It's self-explanatory – give it all to God! I threw away so many documents I had written up, crossed off a bunch of locations on the map, and cried many tears in letting go of each option along the way. But all those things had to be done to enter a true place of surrender.

Space

- A friend and spiritual director a few years back showed me his time management process. Part of it was to plan in what he called 'buffer time.' This was a block of time that he planned from week to week, a time for nothing to happen. He could then use that time how he pleased when it arrived. I've used this technique for productivity purposes too over the years and it has served me well.

- In a similar way, I have found making room for space throughout the Scouting Pattern is essential for wellbeing, longevity, creativity and dreaming. I've noticed that if I am constantly switched on to this pattern (without the space), that my creativity and sense of fun and enjoyment in the process can quickly diminish.

- It's often in the spaces between, in the mulling it over phase that I hear from God most and ideas flourish! I'm finding myself more and more engaged with contemplative times of prayer for this very reason. It's all too easy to let the Planter activist DNA take over in our prayer life.

- This space also gives us room to reflect regularly. I've found this to be incredibly useful. Whether you're an internal or external processor, you can use this space to reflect by yourself or with a friend. Within this reflection space I've been able to spot mistakes I've made along the way or even solve problems that I would have otherwise been overwhelmed by.

- Essentially, by getting out the way and giving the Spirit space to move and breathe in us really helps! Turns out, we're not alone in this process and that it's OK to invite the Spirit and trust others into the pattern.

Scouting as a Daily Pattern in Other Areas of Life

Personally, over the last three years, I've found that going through this pattern as a process has been as much about distilling my calling to leadership and seeking God's will in life as it has in scouting for a place to plant/revitalise a church.

It has become part of my rhythmic discernment, keeping myself in check and hopefully in line with the Spirit and His leading. Again, it's nothing new or profound – dozens of books and talks would have covered all the stages in the pattern and would have done far better than I could ever hope to. This is simply what has developed as one of those small helpful patterns that has got me through some murky waters and will hopefully continue to help me process ministry and be faithful to God's call going forward.

Part of this ongoing process has been to weave the practice of the scouting pattern into other areas of my life. This is still a work in progress, but I have now included it within my journaling time. So, within my journal I have made a template of prompts helping me to rhythmically reflect on the stages of the pattern.

An example of this could be:

1. Where do you need to seek God's guidance today?

2. What steps do you need to take to act on God's prompting?

3. How can you sow into that which you are being led into?

4. Is there anything you need to surrender to God before moving forward?

5. Have you made space for the Spirit to move and for you to catch a breath?

These could be part of your daily rhythm in journaling/reflection or perhaps a prompt at the start of each week. You could even go the whole hog and break it up into daily, weekly, monthly, and yearly points of reflection, specific to your planting/ revitalisation journey or just life in general – make it your own.

Praying the Scouting Pattern

My prayers are often instinctive or based upon what's happening in life. As such they're not always that structured, which is fine. Silence and waiting on the Lord is more powerful than any prayer that I could pray. At times I do like a structure, a liturgy even! I've had a go at writing a very simple prayer to help gather my thoughts for the pattern, but I'd advise making your own version that's applicable to your DNA and context (if writing out prayers is even your thing!).

Scouting Pattern Prayer

Father,
Guide me as I seek Your will,
I know the corruption and ambitions of my heart all too well,
steer me to what You have in store,
keep me from the slippery slope of selfish gain and ugly accomplishment.

Jesus,
As I attempt to join in with what You have prepared,
Help me to follow Your footsteps,
Light the way ahead and magnetise my feet to Your way.
Keep me from boastfully trailblazing, and,
Let my steps be that of peace,
Treading with humility as I enter this new space.

As I invest and sow into a way forward,
Protect my heart, soul, mind and strength,
Give me a soft heart and a sound mind,
As I pour out from the grace You have given me,
For the task ahead — help me to work diligently and vulnerably.

For all that I am holding onto,
Help me to surrender it today.
Even if all of this is in vain,
May it be in vain for You.
May the success or failure of this journey,
Be an act of worship to You.
Bless me with the humility and holiness needed,
To surrender it all to You again and again.

Spirit,
Help me to get out of the way.
Give me a holy awareness of Your presence,
An ability to declutter my activity and,
To simply rest in Your presence.
Grant me the patience to wait on You,
To hear Your voice,
To be still,
To make space for You,
Amen.

Chapter 2
Scaffolding; Forming Foundations and Connections

1 Corinthians 3:9–15

9'For we are co-workers in God's service; you are God's field, God's building. 10 By the grace God has given me, I laid a foundation as a wise builder, and someone else is building on it. But each one should build with care. 11 For no one can lay any foundation other than the one already laid, which is Jesus Christ. 12 If anyone builds on this foundation using gold, silver, costly stones, wood, hay or straw, 13 their work will be shown for what it is, because the Day will bring it to light. It will be revealed with fire, and the fire will test the quality of each person's work. 14 If what has been built survives, the builder will receive a reward. 15 If it is burned up, the builder will suffer loss but yet will be saved – even though only as one escaping through the flames.

Not long after I accepted the 'church revitalisation plant leader' role in Coventry, did I start to spiral into a 'what if?' headspace. For at least three days straight I had an anxious knot in my stomach about the job I'd be taking on and was bombarded by self-inflicted questions that were keeping me up at night. They were questions like,

What if the existing congregation that we graft into doesn't get on board with the changes I make?[5]
What if I'm no good at it?
What if the whole thing is a nightmare?
What if I don't get on with the church wardens?
What if I'm horrible at change management?
What if they're all against me?!
What if I can't manage all the different strands to the role?!
What if no one comes with us from the resource church?
What if the kids don't settle into their new school?
What if Hayley (my wife) can't stand the area?
What if I don't have a team?
What if I can't see a vision for the place?
What if we go bust financially?
What if no one comes to faith?
What if I let everyone down?
What if the church isn't healthy?
What if the church doesn't grow?
What if it's all too much?!

---

[5] A lot of these 'what if?' questions hover around the theme of expectations of others and how I might be perceived. Expectations that we put on ourselves as well as those from other people can be dangerous in this line of work, I've found, because when what we do is led by people's expectations, we limit our expectations of what God can do. I've needed to keep re-aligning myself to make sure that I keep the main thing the main thing and not get derailed by others' expectations along the way.

What if I feel trapped and claustrophobic in the role? What if?! What if?! What if?![6]

Then one evening as I was walking the dog and praying, or rather pleading with God to help me with the noise in my head fuelling this anxiety build up, I was stopped in my tracks next to a house. It was an ordinary house that I'd walked past hundreds of times, but it now had scaffolding all around it. Ordinarily, scaffolding isn't something that would catch my attention; however, I could not take my eyes off it. It was as if the Holy Spirit had locked my gaze upon this house and the scaffolding that was embracing it. So, I stood and waited, bemused by the presence of God found in the waiting and gazing upon this scaffolded house. Perplexed (as is often the case with me) I prayed, asking Jesus, "What are you saying? What do You want me to see here?"

Just as those words left my lips I saw and heard what the Lord was saying, and He was telling me, showing me even, to – 'Scaffold!'

Scaffold. As I understand it, you can't properly build or make changes to a structure without ensuring the necessary scaffolding is in place first. The scaffolding is needed primarily to ensure that: the site is safe,

---

[6] Since writing this and getting into the habit of journaling and learning to give thanks more readily for God's goodness in my life, I have found that a good way to combat the future worry of 'what if…?' is to start with the past hope of 'God has…' Reminding myself of all the promises God has kept over the years, not just for me but to others I know, and of course those in the Bible, has been a helpful way of getting perspective when the 'What if?' storm of questions gets too much.

that workers have access and a better position to work, as well as support for the existing structure and materials being used. That's the construction side of scaffolding, but in education, scaffolding is also a technique often used in teaching. Scaffolding in education gives the learner a model by which they can solve a problem themselves having been given a demonstration and the subsequent support following it.

Whilst standing there observing this house with its scaffolding, it dawned on me that before I could go in making any changes, building a team, starting new missional work etc., I needed to create a scaffold. Before any of the repair work, before any of the building, before any of the 'revitalisation' aspect of the work could happen, I needed to create a 'scaffolding' around this church that I was going to graft into.

At its core, I felt the Lord say that this 'scaffold' was to be a 'relationship'. The thing that was going to provide the safety, support, position, access and model for revitalisation and planting to happen in this place were relationships! These included relationships with the existing church congregation, with people in the resource church that was sending us out, with other clergy in the deanery (including the Area Dean, Archdeacons and Bishops) and of course, relationship with the community that we were trying to reach!

As this sunk in, the 'What if?' questions that were swirling around began to dissipate as I felt reassured that I didn't have to have it all sorted on day one, or even day one hundred! I didn't need to have all the strategy, or all the answers, or to even 'achieve' church growth, because at the end of the day, it's God's job to build His church. I'm simply there (trying to be faithful) to build relationships and point people towards a relationship with Him.

To begin with, all I need to focus on is the 'scaffold'; the relationships. Whilst this is what I felt the Lord was saying for me to focus on primarily in my first year of planting, seven weeks into the job, I found myself wondering if that should be the focus for the entirety of my work here. If I'm to truly embrace the truth, which is that God will build His church, then maybe all I'm ever meant to do is put up the scaffolding. What if the real question I should be asking myself is 'What if you let God build His church, rather than trying to be God, Paul?'

For me this has been an important question to keep coming back to, especially when the driven side of my personality goes into overdrive. Repeatedly in my first year I found myself wanting to 'do more': to set up more initiatives in the church, to start more activities, to organise, to change, change and change some more. But every time I wanted to press the 'turbo' button and ramp up the speed, that word 'scaffold' just popped back in. Sometimes, God would have to lay it on thick and I would see more houses near where we lived have scaffolding put up! I kid you not, the number of houses that suddenly started having scaffolding around them near our property in the first term of moving to Coventry was ridiculous! I'm not so narcissistic to think that God prompted those people to attend to building work on their homes to get through my thick skull, but the timing of their building projects certainly helped me.

One of the hardest things in this phase has been to accept the fact that this initial 'scaffolding' is realistically going to take at least one to two years. I have found myself constantly holding back. It's like having to choose to put yourself in a straitjacket sometimes – that's the only way I can describe the frustration of self-inflicted restraint from bringing change or new things too soon. Something that has helped me to be patient with this scaffolding process and trust God a little bit more, is a word of encouragement I was given after a prayer meeting. The picture shared with me was of angels running around the area and around the churches that we were revitalising: they were arranging things for the church and team in the background, getting things in order, paving the way for myself and others to come in and carry on with the work there. This was such an encouragement as it reminded me that God is in control, that this time for 'scaffolding' is necessary and timely and that God was going ahead of me. Within a couple of weeks of receiving that word from one person, I got another word from a different friend who had a picture of an egg factory and all the machines placing all the different sized eggs in their correct cartons. The interpretation was that God was getting things ordered, placing all the right people and props in the correct positions for the work we were about to embark on. Again, the Spirit was reminding me of the importance of this preparatory relational work and the need to scaffold ahead of the contractional work of revitalisation to come.

Even so, I have still found it so tricky trying to hold back from wanting to implement things in the life of the church, rather than solely focusing on relationship building (Yes, I am incredibly impatient and must learn patience daily!). Is this because I've been exposed to too many 'programmes' in church over the years? Is it because I'm afraid of real discipleship or am just no good at it? Is it that I know deep down that my ego will be more inflated if I get a few quick wins that look good outwardly rather than doing the hard graft of slow one-to-one work?

Each time this gets difficult, I've found myself asking the question 'Why am I finding it hard to hold back and focus on relationships alone?' And often, it comes back to my own insecurity, not trusting that God is going to do what He wants to do regardless of my pace or achievement and my own sense of pride or worth. Yes, it's OK to be passionate and have vision and see an end goal, but if this foundational relationship work isn't put in, then it will only cause problems later. The scaffold needs to be secure, and trust takes time to build. When we moved here, ironically, we needed scaffolding to be put up on our new house for work to be done as it had deteriorated over the years. The Holy Spirit locked my gaze once again upon this scaffolding word.

Firstly, I observed that it took several workers, two full working days to erect the scaffolding, but only a few men less to tear the whole thing down in less than half a day! As I processed this, I heard the Spirit say that the same timing goes for your relationships too. He said, "It can take a long time, with a lot of hard graft to build the scaffolding of trust in your relationships needed here, Paul. But it only takes moments for that trust to be torn down. So, scaffold well!"

The second thing the Holy Spirit was taking me to task on through our home's scaffolding was the scaffolding that I needed. In that moment of gazing upon our own scaffolding, I realised that as I'm trying to build scaffolding in relationship with others, that God is simultaneously putting scaffolding up around me and my heart to prepare and continuously mould me for the job at hand. I often heard people say that prior to entering leadership, you need to make sure that you've 'sorted your stuff out', because it will catch up with you if you don't. Whilst I understand and agree that we should be self-aware enough to deal with things as much as possible prior to entering a leadership role, I think a lot of the work gets done on the job. The important thing is having the necessary scaffolding in place to deal with it as you go so that you don't come crumbling down during the potential storm.

Something I think is a strength of mine is being a learner; to be taught. With that, I have followed all the advice I've been taught when it comes to belt-and-braces care for yourself as a leader. I follow all the steps given, i.e. accountability groups, prayer groups, reading regularly, praying, reading my Bible, retreats etc. But you know, even though all that stuff is in place, from time to time, this job gets gritty and I'm not sure anything can truly prepare you for the accelerated growth and discipleship needed in those moments when you receive a crushing blow and sometimes, its knock after knock, day after day, week after week. It's been in those moments that I am thankful for the word 'scaffolding'. Because through the ministering of the Spirit through that word, I have been able to accept the fact that God is working on my heart daily and often I'm up and about doing the work of a priest whilst God performs open heart surgery. It's vulnerable and it hurts.

But as painful as it is at times, I know I need that scaffolding put in place because even as I diarise these thoughts, I find myself praying for a bigger and softer heart for those I serve, for those who criticise, for those who disagree with church planting/revitalisation, for those who don't understand why I do things the way I do, for myself, and for God, that I would be able to love Him more (because I simply don't love Jesus enough).

I have never felt so exposed and vulnerable as I have since stepping into my role as a church revitalisation plant leader. Sometimes it feels that with every step comes a new piece of scaffolding – the learning curve is that steep at times. And yet, I love that it's keeping me on my knees, because I'm having to cling on to Jesus and His Word more than ever before. I'm appreciating the small wins in ministry and life in general, things I would not have taken the time to rejoice over in the past but now I do because

I see the fragility of it all. This scaffolding process, the business of relationship building is so delicate, especially when church planting – so fragile and yet so flabbergastingly beautiful at the same time!

When trying to get permission to launch a church plant project previously in my Curacy, it felt like one battle after the other. It was a repetitive pattern of feeling like I had to justify and defend planting and this season of my calling to church leadership in the Church of England. This played on loop for three years. Admittedly this was two-sided, and I probably brought as many weapons to the table as those I conversed with. If I faced those conversations now, I would handle them very differently... hindsight.

I realised that when I stepped into my new role (whilst trying to scaffold) that I still had this battle loop playing in my thought processes and in anticipating conversations with various people in church or the deanery. This was problematic because it meant that I was entering those conversations with a battle cry at the ready, meaning that there was adrenalin pumping, an expectation of attrition, a bracing for pain, even defeat, defences to be up, and a sense of fear fuelling emotions. But after a few conversations with different people, I realised that they were not there for a battle – a little confused and apprehensive perhaps, but not battle. It became clear to me that I had entered this project 'battle worn' and conditioned for attrition. Thick skin is fine but becomes problematic when it callouses the heart; being braced for battle makes it hard to embrace blessing.

With that I had to change my perspective when entering conversations and meetings from 'battle' to 'blessing'. Instead of communicating from a stance of battle, I tried to do so with a posture of blessing: not only to try and bless the other person somehow, but to have hope and a positive attitude that they may bless me and that I can learn from them. This changed my outlook and heart direction and meant that I could enter what felt like big meetings with a liberated sense of not having to think that I had to win or prove a point, but instead to simply honour, bless and navigate with the other person.

This has helped me to be more vulnerable in these conversations, to actively listen more carefully and to present ideas passionately but without an insecure need to feel like I had to convince the other person to get on board. Essentially, with a posture of blessing at the forefront, it frees up more room for grace, patience and understanding in potentially difficult meetings; in particular change-oriented meetings.

For the planter I think it can be all too easy and tempting to treat challenges or people as 'battles', because it helps us justify our points of view, takes the blame off our mistakes or shortcomings and gives a false sense of righteousness and heroism that inflates our fragile egos. More reason, I think, to focus on how the other person is a blessing to God and us, and how we need to work harder to be a blessing towards them – especially when so much of what we bring involves cultural change and restructuring.

I have found that as a planter entering a new space or trying to pave the way for new ground, we tend to start from a minus number on the scale of good relations. Therefore, we, more so than others in church leadership, need to work our socks off in being a genuine blessing to those we interact with and seek to build good relationships with. We cannot do that if we are applying war paint every morning and arming ourselves for a fight whilst listening to amped up worship songs. To go out and bless, to build safe and secure scaffold connections with others, we must strip ourselves of the defences and weapons that try to protect our wounded hearts and petty egos and instead clothe ourselves with humility, gentleness, and love – that's how we bring peace to troubled hearts and minds and that's how we provide the safe and secure scaffolding connections needed to hold this project together as we set out to build!

Matthew 5:9
"Blessed are the peacemakers, for they will be called children of God."

Scaffolding Prayer

Jesus, as I set out into the unknown,
Help me to see what You want me to see,
Keep my pace steady, moving in sync with Your Spirit.
Heal me of past hurt that has calloused my heart and clouded my mind,
Teach me to see others as You see them,

To acknowledge the blessing that they are to You and can be to me.

Give me a bigger, softer heart, so that I too may be a blessing to those I meet.

Where fear and pride has braced me for battle mistakenly,

Replace it with humility, gentleness, and love, so that I may know Your peace,

and bring peace to others as I go.

Father, help me to live as Your child,

In the comfort of Your embrace and trust of Your good and perfect will for my life and ministry,

Amen.

Journaling Point

So, to wrap this chapter up, I thought I'd jot down a few questions that I've been asking myself as I go and learn. Here they are:

- Holy Spirit, what do You want me to see here?

- Am I finding it hard to hold back and focus on relationships alone? If so, why is that happening?

- How am I getting in the way of God's plans?

- Where does my heart need to become bigger and softer?

- What track do I have playing on repeat in my mind?

- Am I entering this project/meeting/conversation with a perspective of battle or blessing?

- Am I bringing war or peace to this context?

Chapter 3
Shaping; Allowing God to Shape the Church and Me

Isaiah 64:8
"Yet you, Lord, are our Father. We are the clay, You are the Potter; we are all the work of Your hand."

Psalm 127:1–2
Unless the Lord builds the house, the builders labour in vain. Unless the Lord watches over the city, the guards stand watch in vain. In vain you rise early and stay up late, toiling for food to eat – for He grants sleep to those He loves.

Matthew 16:17–18b
"Jesus replied... I will build My church..."

Pottery and Pruning

A few years ago, Hayley and I took a pottery class whilst on holiday. I was amazed at just how difficult it was to shape this little lump of clay! There were so many things to think about all at once; the pace of the spinning wheel that the clay sat on, the amount of water to add in as it spun, how much pressure to apply to the clay and constantly thinking through the next stage of what it would look like as you were shaping it from its previous form into the current one. I think church planting is a bit like this pottery process. You start with this lump of clay and try to shape it the best you can with all these different mechanics going on as you constantly evolve and shape this growing thing. In the place we're in, our church plant is a graft, so our clay already has an existing shape. So, in our case, we are adding clay to the existing shape and reshaping both the new and the old together into a new shape. Did I mention that pottery is also messy.

In a church plant-graft project like ours, I'm realising that this merging process of two lumps of clay is an incredibly sensitive and fragile process: too much pressure on the clay and it misshapes; not enough pressure and it becomes stagnant and stuck; too much water and it thins out; too little and the clay is unmoldable; too fast and it spins out of control flying everywhere; too slow and it loses flexibility.

Our plant project isn't a blank canvas one, where you've got a fresh sheet, no inherited traditions and you can run with every idea under the sun. Ours is a revitalisation project. It's a plant-graft, so we've inherited people, traditions and a culture (a lot of which is wonderful and fruitful), but there are times where it clashes with the new. And so, we have two bits of clay being blended, and sometimes it gets messy.[7]

There's an expression in church planting that planting is like trying to build a plane whilst it's flying. I think that's true for a blank canvas plant, but when you're trying to build and shape a graft project that needs revitalisation, I think a more fitting analogy is that it's more like getting on to a raft and trying to plug all the holes so that you don't drown, whilst also trying to put a sail up and paddle! It means, the church – the raft – is already out at sea, with some residual movement from its past. However, it's got signs of wear and tear and water coming in that needs addressing. At the same time, you're trying to assemble the sail so that you can catch the right wind and move in the right direction. All the while,

---

[7] A few months back I was watching one of these home design programmes and in this episode, they were attempting to rebuild/ revitalise a house in the forest and doing so out of what already existed within the forest. They did it this way because they didn't want it to be something alien to its surroundings; they wanted the house to have both the existing DNA and feel of the forest it would be situated in, but they also needed to bring in new supplies and work to achieve that. So, what they did, and I think this is beautiful, was to take the stonework that was already part of the old building and forest area and then they took the new brick work and blended it around the old. And what they ended up having was both the existing stonework/bricks with the new bricks grafted in to create an entirely new structure. It was still true to what it was before within the context of the forest. Isn't that a beautiful image – to see past and present grafted together in that way to create something new for the future? That really spoke to me about how to approach our plant-graft here. I suppose it's another way of seeing the two clumps of clay being moulded together, but when I get a bit off track with how things are panning out, little images like this help me to realign how we go about doing things.

you need to paddle to keep everything going and at times you're going against the current and at times you're moving with it – it's unpredictable! Essentially, whether you're in a plane or on a raft, both forms of planting are challenging and come with their own unique highs and lows.

I've needed a lot of heart shaping and re-moulding in order to embrace that, because I think I had anticipated it looking like one shape, when in fact God seems to be doing something different. I've needed to and will continue to need to be pliable for His purposes, whilst holding to the right convictions. It's a tricky balance to strike right and I often get it wrong and create another hole in the raft.

It's easy in a grafting project like this to wrongly assume that we must clear away everything that was there before so that we can start with a blank canvas. But to treat people and their history and, more importantly, the work of the Holy Spirit over the years in this way would be a careless mistake. I really hope I'm not doing this with the changes I'm trying to initiate and re-mould into this place; sadly, it wouldn't surprise me if I have messed up in this way at some point in the journey. God really spoke to me about this before we moved here. It was a sunny day and I decided to finally get to work on an overgrown hedge that was taking over the garden. It was time to prune!

With a mission to accomplish I went to town with the chainsaw and completely took down the bulk of this hedge, leaving only what was necessary. There wasn't an angle or direction that the chainsaw didn't go to trim this thing. By the end of it, it felt good to look back at the newly trimmed hedge, which now allowed the sunlight to beam through into the garden. Not long after this, I noticed a bird going back and forth from it. Curious as to why, I went to inspect my work and noticed that there was a bird's nest hidden within, with baby chicks residing! I couldn't believe it! There I was, slashing away at this hedge, cutting every which way and somehow, by the grace of God I managed to miss these chicks. Thank goodness! Once I'd processed my literal close shave, I began to reflect on it considering the church plant-graft we were about to take on and sensed the Holy Spirit warning me not to go into this place with a chainsaw of change spinning round the place; but rather to recognise that within this hedge there was new life (It wasn't life that I had created or done anything to facilitate. If anything, my interaction almost killed it off!). All my interaction did was to unveil the life and beauty that was already growing there. I could have so easily destroyed something special that was organically forming. The positive was that I had trimmed this hedge and now was aware of this wonderful life that was growing within it, however I had also now exposed that life to predators and the elements (and had almost killed it in the process). So, I had to place a bit of branch protection around it to fend off the cat that prowled the fence.

It could have been a disaster with those chicks. By the grace of God, they continued to grow and live on, despite my clumsiness. Pioneering work can be clumsy. We can get carried away initiating the new thing, and, if we're not careful, we can forget that the existing thing has beauty and life too. That's got me thinking an awful lot about the distinction between being a pastor and a pioneer and what those terms mean and look like in a church plant-graft process. Because, if we are going to re-mould this clay, combining the old with the new, to form something for the future, then we need to be pioneering pastorally. I think we do ourselves a disservice as planters if we label ourselves as either only pastor or only pioneer. I think we need to be OK with holding the tension of being both; we're no less a pastor if we drive change and momentum from time to time, and we're no less a pioneer if we step back and take the time to listen, learn from and care for our flock. If we rush this, we run the risk of not knowing our flock's voice and they misunderstand ours; and even worse, not knowing Jesus' voice amid all the hustle and bustle of the day to day.

God the Potter

When it comes to the day to day, I have found myself continuously getting in the way of the Spirit and trying to control everything. My perfectionist streak rears its head and wants to keep everything tidy and tight, with no room for error or meandering; but the "wind blows wherever it pleases. You hear its sound, but you cannot tell where it comes from or where it is going. So, it is with everyone born of the Spirit."[8] With that I find myself revisiting the Scouting Pattern and having to learn the art of surrender repeatedly throughout this journey.

Not long ago I did a brief study into Luke 1, which has now become one of my favourite chapters in the Bible, because it completely shatters the box we so often try to contain God in. For me, so much of this chapter shouts out the art of surrender and the importance of it as we navigate not just church planting and the shape our churches take, but also our own discipleship and shaping as followers of Jesus. As such, I find it to be an incredibly liberating chapter for us to engage with as Spirit-filled Christians and it often makes me chuckle as I read through it.

I find it comforting because it reminds me that God is boss and that I don't need to take myself too seriously. It reminds me that God is in control and that He is going to do what He wants to do through the work of His Spirit and that I just need to ride that wave and join in with Him where I can on this crazy rollercoaster that is church planting. Before moving on I think it's worth unpacking this just a little, considering how we can learn to allow God, as Potter, to shape the church and surrender to His plans along the way...

Read what it says in this chapter:

---

[8] John 3:8

'5In the time of Herod king of Judea, there was a priest named Zechariah, who belonged to the priestly division of Abijah; his wife Elizabeth was also a descendant of Aaron. 6 Both of them were righteous in the sight of God, observing all the Lord's commands and decrees blamelessly. 7 But they were childless because Elizabeth was not able to conceive, and they were both very old.

8 Once when Zechariah's division was on duty and he was serving as priest before God, 9 he was chosen by lot, according to the custom of the priesthood, to go into the temple of the Lord and burn incense. 10 And when the time for the burning of incense came, all the assembled worshipers were praying outside.

11 Then an angel of the Lord appeared to him, standing at the right side of the altar of incense. 12 When Zechariah saw him, he was startled and was gripped with fear. 13 But the angel said to him: "Do not be afraid, Zechariah; your prayer has been heard. Your wife Elizabeth will bear you a son, and you are to call him John. 14 He will be a joy and delight to you, and many will rejoice because of his birth, 15 for he will be great in the sight of the Lord. He is never to take wine or other fermented drink, and he will be filled with the Holy Spirit even before he is born.'

Baby John, before he's even born, whilst in his mother's womb, is filled with the Holy Spirit? WHAT?!

But he's an unborn child – how does he accept Jesus into his life? How does he choose to journey with Jesus? How does he join the church? He's not even born and he's filled with the Holy Spirit... what?!

Then, if that wasn't enough for us to try and comprehend, listen to this:

> '39At that time, Mary got ready and hurried to a town in the hill country of Judea,40 where she entered Zechariah's home and greeted Elizabeth. 41 When Elizabeth heard Mary's greeting, the baby leaped in her womb, and Elizabeth was filled with the Holy Spirit. 42 In a loud voice she exclaimed: "Blessed are you among women, and blessed is the child you will bear!"'

I bet it was a loud voice!

Mary shows up with Jesus in her womb. She walks into Elizabeth's house, and from simply hearing Mary come through the door, her unborn, spirit-filled baby jumps for joy in her womb and then Elizabeth is filled with the Holy Spirit too! What?!

I mean, she didn't even hold her hands out to receive the Spirit! She didn't say or recite any prayers, go for confirmation classes, or attend any special ceremonies... It was just 'boom', the baby jumped because the unborn Jesus entered the house and then, 'boom', the Holy Spirit filled her unannounced! This is bonkers! It completely shatters the box which we often try to put God in, doesn't it?

Then to top it all off, you've got John's dad, Zechariah, who became a mute as a punishment for second guessing that God would bless him with a child. So understandably, Zechariah was a bit sceptical about God giving him a miracle baby. Zechariah was trying to put rules and expectations around God, he was trying to box in the Holy Spirit and God punished him for it. This is serious stuff. So anyway, Zechariah's a mute now for trying to box up God, and then whilst living with this punishment out of nowhere we read, '*67His father Zechariah was filled with the Holy Spirit and prophesied.'*[9] Boom! Another one! Out of nowhere, with no warning, with no process or programme, he gets hit with the Spirit and is catapulted into prophesying over baby John's life after being mute... What?!

And let's not forget the instigator of all these spirit-filled events – Jesus! It was Jesus and the immaculate conception, a baby birthed within the virgin Mary. If you hadn't picked up on the point yet, let me spell it out: God is bigger than all our church plant plans! At the end of the day, the Holy Spirit is going to do what He wants to do; He cannot be boxed in. No matter how hard we try to organise the Spirit, the Spirit moves whichever way He pleases, and we simply need to surrender to His will.

---

[9] Luke 1:67

That's what Mary did. She said, *'38 "I am the Lord's servant," Mary answered. "May Your word to me be fulfilled." Then the angel left her.*[10]

'Let it be.' That in a nutshell holds all the other statements made here on surrender.

The Holy Spirit wants to miraculously help a barren woman get pregnant; let it be.

The Holy Spirit wants to fill the unborn baby John; let it be.

The Holy Spirit wants to cause an unborn baby to leap with joy; let it be.

The Holy Spirit wants to silence Zechariah; let it be.

The Holy Spirit wants to bless Zechariah with a prophetic word even though he'd been sinful before; let it be.

The Holy Spirit wants to anoint Mary with the birth of God; let it be.

The Holy Spirit wants to completely turn your church plant plans upside down and inside out; let it be!

Ultimately, it's about 'surrender' to God, isn't it?

Surrendering what we think the plan is.
Surrendering what we think God should be doing.
Surrendering what we think should be done.
Surrendering our defences.
Surrendering our grudges.
Surrendering our fears and anxieties.
Surrendering even our hopes.

---

[10] Luke 1:38

Back in my Curacy, after three years of trying to force a church plant to birth and at times getting close, we then lost it. Having failed repeatedly, I cried out to God and said 'Fine! I've tried to make something happen and it's not working, so I give it to You. Take it.'

And I simply surrendered all the plans I had made over those three years to God.

Documents that had been written over the years torn up; charts and plans on the computer that I had poured over I simply moved into the archives. The map of the area on the wall with drawing pins and dreams in it, pulled down. Books on church planting thrown to the side. The Church planting podcast I created was put on hold. In this area of life and leadership I'd simply come to the end of myself and essentially, I said to God, 'let it be.'

I had finally relented and surrendered the plans to God. For three years I was butting heads with Him, trying to box the Spirit into my plans, what I wanted, where I wanted. And God humbled me.

1 Peter 5:1–7 says this:

'To the elders among you, I appeal as a fellow elder and a witness of Christ's sufferings who also will share in the glory to be revealed: 2 Be shepherds of God's flock that is under your care, watching over them – not because you must, but because you are willing, as God wants you to be; not pursuing dishonest gain, but eager to serve; 3 not lording it over those entrusted to you,

*but being examples to the flock. **4** And when the Chief Shepherd appears, you will receive the crown of glory that will never fade away.**5** In the same way, you who are younger, submit yourselves to your elders. All of you, clothe yourselves with humility toward one another, because, "God opposes the proud but shows favour to the humble." **6** Humble yourselves, therefore, under God's mighty hand, that He may lift you up in due time. **7** Cast all your anxiety on Him because He cares for you.'*

Surrendering to God and being taken down a notch or two by Him (like Zechariah was) when we need to be humbled is a funny thing, isn't it? On the one hand, it is so overwhelming and scary because we suddenly get a glimpse into the might of God, but then at the same time, amid that fear of God, He so tenderly holds us. In that moment of surrender and eating 'humble pie', under His mighty hand we feel the weight of God's presence, but at the same time, we know that He will lift us up again.

The act of surrender is so surreal in that way. Whilst we go through the pain of being humbled, we go through the joy of being held. And in this chapter of Luke, we see all that surrender and joy. And amid that surrender, what do we see? We see joy and we see life. As hard and as testing that act of surrender is, as difficult and costly as it can be to utter the words 'let it be', the joy and the life that is birthed out of it is more than we could ever imagine or measure, isn't it?

The joy of the Spirit at work in a person's life, when we witness that transformation in someone, when we witness Jesus at work in our own life or the life of someone who has come to know Him, that is joy. When we see people living life to the full in Christ, that's life giving, isn't it? The waiting of pregnancy, the pains of labour, they're worth it for the joy and life that come about as a result.

It's my prayer that we would see the Spirit do what He wants in this church plant.
It's my prayer that He would do in me what He wants to do.
It's my prayer that we as a church would live lives of surrender to Jesus.
It's my prayer that the people here would know the joy and life of Jesus in their lives and that we would be able to point them towards that.
Let it be so, Lord Jesus – Potter, come and shape us!

Being the Clay

I think one of the main things I'm learning from this planting experience is that out of everything that needs shaping, I'm the one in most desperate need of God to come and re-shape me; to re-shape my stony heart. A few months into this role and the harsh realisation that I am incredibly insecure on so many levels have well and truly kicked in: not to mention my lack of compassion and grace on a day-to-day basis. It's great having a vision to see great missional work taking place in the area we are serving, but it means little if our heart posture is out of sync with God's.

There is no point trying to live out this planting lark if we cannot cultivate a heart of compassion for those we have picked up along the way. There's no point trying to reach the lost if we cannot even love those who are already in front of us. The father with a demon-possessed child in Mark's gospel said to Jesus, 'But if you can do anything, take pity on us and help us.'[11] Compassion was the posture from which Jesus exercised His power in prayer. If we are to plant churches, then our posture is to be one of compassion; compassion for the lost and the church.

Groundbreaking mission starts with God breaking ground in us. Our relationship with Him and aligning our heart desires to His is paramount, because in those moments where we get cross and frustrated, we have two choices: Our frustration can either transform into vision or if we let it, it can turn into venom. How we feed this emotion will determine which transformation takes place. Hence the importance of allowing ourselves to be daily shaped by Jesus Christ, taking time out of the day to be with Him and getting our hearts and minds in check before Him (especially when things are tricky).

I'm ashamed to say that I used to turn my nose up at those who said things like, 'If all you do is pray all day, then that is enough.' The more the days go on, the more aware I am that I have neglected prayer

---

[11] Mark 9:22b

and placed pragmatism and activism above pursuing the presence of God. Sadly, I think this pursuit of achievement and getting things done has hardened my heart somewhat to people and the Lord. Too often I have caught myself not looking with eyes of mercy, but with eyes of judgement or frustration. I wonder what ministry would look like if I looked at people with eyes that genuinely loved them. In trying to be what I think a 'planter' should be, have I forgotten that I am a priest, a deacon, a husband, a father, a child of God?

I think one of the reasons why I have found planting so hard at times is because I am being forced to confront these insecurities and frailties I have whilst at the same time trying to live out the job. It forces you to be vulnerable, not just to those around you, but to God also in allowing him to be the Potter and you the clay.

And it's not just about allowing God to shape us in this process either. In coming into this church and grafting in, at first, I was focusing on what DNA I was bringing to the table. I was thinking about how what I was bringing was going to shape things round here. But as the months have gone on and I have allowed myself to soften, I have realised that it's just as much about allowing myself to be shaped by the existing church here and the community around it. As I bring in my own DNA to shape things, I am learning to be shaped by them too and their ways. They are teaching me as I attempt to lead them – a mutual cross pollination of understanding one another. And that has been special, and very humbling at times too.

Part of that process has involved God teaching me about Patience and Proximity: patience for myself for when I make mistakes or am not loving enough, and patience for the church. It's easy to want to distance yourself from someone when they hurt you or disagree with you. Whilst on a retreat, the Spirit challenged me on this through John 10 and the Good Shepherd; in particular verse 4b, 'The sheep follow Him because they know His voice.' In reading and praying through this verse and chapter, I realised that my sheep didn't know my voice well enough, because I'd not been drawing close enough to them.

Whether deliberately or as a subconscious defence, I'd been creating distance, and God challenged me on this saying, 'If you are really going to love My church, then you need to get closer to her; and you need to get closer to Me if you're going to do that.' It was a stern challenge and I spent half of my retreat repenting of not loving the church well enough and for harbouring anger, and secondly, for not pressing into Jesus more, as I so often try to do it alone. There's no point planting churches if we can't love people and if we can't receive the love of God for ourselves daily. We're not here to please people or be liked by people, but we can love them, and that takes patience and proximity.

Seeing the way the apostle Paul addresses the church in his letters, reminds me time and time again of my need to grow in love for the church and to allow myself to be truly vulnerable to her so that I may love her more wholeheartedly. In years gone by, my prayer has always been, 'Lord break my heart for the lost!' It remains that, but added to that now is, 'Lord break my heart for Your church too!' After all, Jesus says that it's by this love for the church that those outside of it will know we are His followers:

John 13:34–35

34'A new command I give you: Love one another. As I have loved you, so you must love one another. 35 By this everyone will know that you are My disciples, if you love one another."

Shaping Prayer

Father, humble me that I would allow You to shape me,
I invite You to be the Potter and I the clay.
Mould me into the person You have called me to be,
for those whom You have called me to serve,
but more importantly, for the child I am in Your arms.
Help me to love Your church with a tender heart,
Not to be harsh with her, but to seek to truly understand and hold her.
Help me not to get in the way of what Your spirit wants to do,
but to simply join in with a 'let it be' attitude.
Shape me to be more like You, Jesus,
Amen.

Journaling Point

- Where does your heart need to soften?

- Have you built up resentment that you need to let go?

- What has shaped you as a planter ahead of you coming into your new planting situation?

- Who are you allowing to shape you as your church plant?

- Where in your life and plant plans do you need to say 'let it be'?

- How are you practising patience?

- Who might you have distanced yourself from that Jesus is prompting you to draw closer to?

PAUL PAVLOU

Chapter 4
Shadows; Shining a Light on the Shadow Side of Planting

Hebrews 12:1–3

'Therefore, since we are surrounded by such a great cloud of witnesses, let us throw off everything that hinders and the sin that so easily entangles. And let us run with perseverance the race marked out for us, fixing our eyes on Jesus, the pioneer and perfecter of faith. For the joy set before Him, He endured the cross, scorning its shame, and sat down at the right hand of the throne of God. Consider Him who endured such opposition from sinners, so that you will not grow weary and lose heart.'

Scattered throughout the 'Snippets' chapter later (chapter six), you will likely see a whole array of disgruntled, raw diary entries from me about how the day has gone, or about something I'm wrestling with, a down or dark day mentally about ministry as well as some brighter and more joy-filled entries. However, in this chapter I wanted to have a go at reflecting on and unpacking some of those 'shadow' side diary snippets I've written, so to help provide some awareness of what may be hindering us in our work to church plant/graft.

The verses above from the book of Hebrews highlight a whole range of things that can stop us from running the race of leadership well; they bring up questions such as:

What hinders us? What sin entangles us?
What causes us to lose our fixation on Jesus?
How do those things demoralise us and deplete our perseverance and joy?
What in our leadership is causing us to become weary or lose heart?

Well for me, so far, there have been three Cs that I've stepped in, that have almost crippled me in leadership and it's still early days!

Those three Cs are: Comparison, Capacity and Criticism.

I'm going to address each of them and what I have since put in place to help navigate such pitfalls as I continue to run the race. Not everything I recount or reflect on here will fit into these three categories, because our emotions and minds are more complicated than that, but hopefully something useful out of the difficulties of this line of work will shine through the shadow aspects of it.

Comparison

So, first C – Comparison.

Galatians 6 warns us of comparison. Verses 4–5 say, *'Each one should test their own actions. Then they can take pride in themselves alone, without comparing themselves to someone else, for each one should carry their own load.'*

In the run up to starting my Curacy, I began to constantly question my own leadership ability, because I was so focused on comparing my leadership to other leaders.

With that comparison being my focus, I quickly went in on myself, like a python, crushing myself and my own self-esteem, because I was so busy focusing on the strength of others, that I had no room left for seeing the strengths God had given me.

Like Galatians says, I was carrying someone else's load, trying to run their race, rather than focusing on my race, and it was weighing me down. This is clearly a destructive behaviour and was contributing to the decline in my mental health.

Towards the end of my Curacy, I thought I had escaped comparison; however, it has only reared its head more since starting my role in Coventry. So often I have caught myself thinking about where I need to get the church to, based on what I've seen other churches do. So often I've given myself deadlines to get things done, because I've seen other people work on similar timescales. Too often I've looked at churches/leaders who are thirty to fifty years ahead of me, thinking that I need to achieve what they've spent a lifetime working on. This type of comparison is toxic, and I have wasted far too many nights and energy during the day stressing about what others have done. It's OK to learn from people, observe the things they've done well and the things they haven't done so well. However, to let that dictate your own trajectory is dangerous.

At times, this kind of deep-rooted comparison has chipped away at my subconscious and how I feel about my calling. It has wormed its way into the point where I have laid awake on many occasions in this first year really questioning whether I am the right man for the job. Because, as I've looked around at other Planters/Revitalisers, I couldn't help but think how brilliant they all were and the incredible gifting and anointing that they carry. As a result, being wired the way I am, I automatically begin to deduce that therefore I could not possibly be called to this place, because I don't feel that I walk with the same skillset or brain to pull this off. Then before you know it, I'm struggling to breath, in a cold sweat, unable to sleep and panicking that I've got this all wrong and have uprooted my family for something far too big for me – and I sink into rumination and self-condemnation about my calling. It becomes a downward spiral – a lot of which (not all) stems from comparison and some from the spiritual battle that exists in our midst.

All that said, I am learning to trust God's decision to put me in this role and as a result, learning to trust my own instincts more rather than looking to what other leaders might do; I'm learning that it's OK to be me and to lead in my own unique way (warts and all) because, at the end of the day, I'm the one who God has called here and my family is the family God has called here. He's given us the space in our hearts to live this out – no one else. So, why waste time comparing it to others?

Capacity

Second C – Capacity.

I've felt called into church leadership for years, and so stepping into it was great, but it came with what felt like a heavy burden. And to a certain extent that can be healthy in that you take the call of God seriously, but as I found out, it can quickly spiral into an unhealthy state.

Being of Greek Cypriot heritage, I tend to load up my plate at mealtime, and this was no different with my work and lifestyle capacity in general.

So onto my plate I piled work; I put on family life with my wife and two kids, exercising intensively daily, getting up super early to study the Bible, going to lots of meetings, fixing all the problems I came across straight away, adding hobbies to the list and so forth, until my plate was piled on with stuff. It's OK to have a little bit of everything on your plate, but when you try to have all of everything all at once, that's where things start going wrong. And it did go wrong. I got physically ill and ended up in A&E on a drip for several days...

My body was giving me warning signs over a deeper problem that had been brewing way before I entered leadership, but leadership was bringing it all to the surface as I would soon find out. In Exodus 31:14a it says 'observe the Sabbath, because it is holy to you. Anyone who desecrates it is to be put to death.' Rest is so important and knowing your capacity to rest well is really helpful. For me, it wasn't so much the amount of work that broke my capacity and rest, although it did play a part, but for me it was two things:

1. The overload of trying to do everything in my life at 100% always;

2. Everything I was doing was being done from a place of comparison and self-criticism. Comparison and criticism are poor choices of fuel for the race of leadership. You will deplete your capacity if it is fuelled on comparison and criticism.

I have to constantly reassess what my current capacity is in this church planting role, and almost daily take stock of what I will allow to stretch my capacity and what I need to pass to someone else or just ignore. What we are called to, really tie into this, and I think we need to see our calling more as a flowing constant that can be moulded into different shapes as the years go on, rather than a fixed solid state. Today's calling may be the work needed to grow us for tomorrow's new capacity, which in turn gives us what we need for the next thing we are called to, and so on. I find the tension of keeping my calling in sync with my capacity a tricky one and I am constantly trying to find the balance between the two.

So, what's your capacity? Are you resting? Are you putting too much of everything on your plate? Are you cutting your race short by fuelling up on the wrong stuff? Are your calling and your capacity in sync?

Criticism

OK, third C – Criticism.

I'm not talking about others criticising me (although that does come with the territory). To give a brief example of how public criticism has affected me, at local conferences, if we have to wear a name badge, I often try to cover it up simply because I don't want people to see my name and think, 'Oh, he's one of the dioceses "church planters". We know what he's about.' I want people to get to know me before judging me based on my job role. Needless to say, I feel incredibly vulnerable now as a church planter, especially at diocesan events. Actually I often dread events like that for this very reason. That being said, people have been very kind to me in my current diocese and the support from people in all manner of positions has been incredible, so I recognise that a lot of this is my own insecurity and brokenness, which I'm working through daily. However, I think it's important to note that being a planter is a vulnerable position and at times lonely because of the baggage/ assumptions it can bring with it. All that being said, what I'm really wanting to highlight is 'self-criticism'.

It's that little voice in your head which puts you down, that tells you that you can't do something, you should be feeling guilty about everything and that you haven't got what it takes. It's that voice that tells you that you'll fail and fall and when you do fall down, that you won't be able to get up again.

Can you identify with that voice?

If you find yourself focusing on being a better Christian rather than becoming more like Jesus, then it's likely that you're prone to self-criticism...

As Christians we are told in the Bible that we have the mind of Christ; that through the work of the Spirit we can make good choices and speak truth over ourselves. I believe in that promise. However, it becomes hard to do that, if we have reached burnout capacity and spend all our time comparing ourselves and wasting all our thoughts on criticising ourselves. When the three c's come together in this way, it's dangerous...

During my Curacy, I was in the middle of a significant wave of depression, because the three Cs had spiralled together and taken hold.

It was a bit like having a suitcase crammed[12] full of clothes and items where you have to sit on it to try and keep it closed at the point where it's ready to burst open any moment. Then when a few circumstantial disappointments came my way, that's exactly what happened: my suitcase of emotions – of

---

[12] This was one of the many helpful analogies my counsellor gave me to help explain what I was doing with my emotions and experiences over the years.

these three Cs built up over the years (and especially during my leadership years) – could not be compressed any longer and it all came flying out and knocked me for six.

I became very depressed. It was an incredibly dark and ugly few months that my family and I lived through as a result. However, due to a few changes and help from others along the way, therapy, support from doctors, a sensational training incumbent and his wife (both of whom I owe an incredible amount to), an incredibly loving church family and lots of prayer, I was gradually able to get up again and to keep running. But it took all those people to help me up again – we cannot do this thing in isolation!

I should probably mention here (and will unpack further on in this chapter) that within my time here, I engaged with more in depth therapy, along with the doctor's support. During this first year of leading the church graft, I have become very aware of how high my anxiety has been, as well as wrestling with depression too. When your wife walks into the room and finds you curled up on the floor in numb despair, it's not a good look. Out of everyone on this planting journey, she is the one that bears the brunt of my low days. It's Hayley who gets the dregs of energy that are left in me after a hard day; who has been there to pick me up when I've not had the energy to even move; who sits and cries with me when it all gets too much; who reminds me of how faithful God has been to us and the incredible privilege it is to be purposed here with the people we're serving and reaching.

And it's Hayley who helped me to see that if I am to continue healthily in leadership, then I need to address my issues head on – the help and work I did during Curacy to get on top of depression was so valuable and got me through, but I am still very much a work in progress. If nothing else, being a church planter has revealed to me just how much I need Jesus and just how incredible my wife is!

Spiritual Criticism

I think it's worth mentioning here under the banner of 'criticism' that this work (as I'm sure you know) is not simply a human effort in our own physical earthly realm. We are very much engaged with a spiritual dimension and just as we are trying to claim ground in the name of Jesus, Satan too is doing his own planting. When we church plant, we are bringing a new culture, a kingdom culture, into an area. Therefore, there is inevitably a clash. One of the first places I think Satan will try to 'sow' as he attempts to 'plant' his own culture into a place, is 'sowing' doubt, fear and criticism into the mind and hearts of those leading the church. I have experienced 'spiritual warfare' before – that thick cloud that seems to be hanging over every part of the day and its conversations, but nothing like I've experienced since stepping into this role. And what has surprised me most is how quickly we were engaging with it!

Not even forty-eight hours in, my wife and I found ourselves in the thick of it. We had tears, fears, doubts and unrest almost immediately over our move here. Things were kicking off around us in the neighbourhood, we felt deeply out of place and genuinely wondered what we had done. For at least four weeks we took it in turns to cry and panic over the decision we had made. We felt uneasy, burdened, irritable and constantly off-centre. Often, these feelings, thoughts, and very often inner criticisms, were unmerited, and then we would realise that Satan was on the attack. In the very early days of moving here, my wife and I found ourselves praying more than we ever had before – it was the only thing we could think to do to fight off all the criticism that was happening in us and to some extent, the events happening around us. Sometimes we would come home from an evening out and we would feel down and heavy, for no human reason, and then, after about an hour of trying to figure it out, we would realise that Satan had been having a dig at us, criticising us from different angles. So we'd pray, and the 'cloud of criticism' would lift.

I haven't spoken anywhere near enough about prayer as I should in my journaling. But as time goes on, I'm realising more and more that it really is the key. I don't think there's any silver bullet in church planting, but I think prayer and worship may be the closest things to one.

So, we have prayer and praise as incredible weapons against the 'shadows' but what are some of the other ways we can counter comparison, capacity and criticism?

Comparison Counter

So, my first C was 'comparison'. So, let's counter that first.

Going back to that Hebrews passage from the start, in verses one and two, it says, 'Let us run with perseverance the race marked out for us, fixing our eyes on Jesus...'

A sure way to end a marathon is with comparison.

The problem with comparison is that you start trying to switch lanes and run the race marked for someone else. In doing so, you're always looking toward what they're doing and focusing on the other, rather than fixing your eyes on Jesus.

You begin to break two of the ten commandments — you covet the strengths and giftings the other person has and to a certain extent you turn them into an idol, because your fixation is on what they can do, rather than what Jesus can do.

When you begin to push the Comparison issue further, you realise that you begin to lose grip of your present reality because you're always looking ahead to the other person's path and future, and you're completely distracted and diverted from the race that God has laid out before you specifically.

To counter Comparison, you've got to be real about where you are today: in your health, spirituality, emotions, capacity etc. You must seek God's face to run your race. When we walk in His presence, we become more content with our present.

When you do that, and when you're real about your present situation and where you are in your planting project, rather than try to be where someone else is in their race, then you begin to see who you are as a leader and what giftings and strengths God has given you specifically, as a fearfully and wonderfully formed person.

So, if Comparison is your thing, then come to Jesus, fix your eyes on Him and learn to be content in His presence...

Capacity Counter

Capacity! What has God given you capacity for?

I've learnt that capacity looks different for everyone and that it is often linked with our strengths and weaknesses. That's why it's so important not to compare, because if you are trying to run like someone else, then you'll soon tire yourself out. What they have capacity for will be different to what you have.

Jesus – and only Jesus – had the capacity to take on the Cross and our sin and shame. He had the capacity to die on the Cross for us and rise back to life because He is God. No one else has the capacity to do that. No one else and nothing else can save us from our sin, because only Jesus has the grace and power capacity needed to do that. That was the race laid out before Him; no one else could run it. Jesus knew the race He had to run because He knew who He was in Father God's eyes. When we lead from a place of being known by God, rather than trying to be God, we learn to be content with our God-given capacity and run our race at the right pace.

So, what's helped me practically to foster a space for working with the capacity I've been given?

A few quick things:

1. Rhythms. Establish your rhythms of prayer, worship, days off, the types of work you do throughout a week. My job is very varied. Where possible, try to spread out the different aspects of your job or life. Accept the busy waves for what they are, but don't forget to ride the waves of a calm season too.

2. Become childlike (after all, Jesus told us to become so in Matthew 18). If you constantly find yourself facing a frown in the mirror, then it's time to find fun. Get a hobby, be silly again – play! Being like a little child again will replenish your capacity and give you perspective about what's important on your To Do list.

    Whilst there's no silver bullet in this work, I'm beginning to think that 'childlikeness' may be a key factor to thriving in the work of church planting. More and more I'm finding the need to surrender and be like a little child again in coming to my Father to ask for help, wisdom, joy, peace, courage, humility etc. More and more I'm finding that I need to rely on Him as Father, rather than thinking that I can run before I can walk. More and more I'm realising that simply falling back into His embrace is enough for me to be 'successful' on any given day.

3. Plan in buffer time. This has been a life saver for me. When you plan your week, plan in one or two slots in that week for absolutely nothing. I've found that having that in place means that I can take comfort in the fact that I will have an extra clear spot in the diary, that I could use for rest/a last minute meeting/catch up/reading/or space for creativity.

Criticism Counter

And lastly – Criticism. How can we combat criticism?

I've found the strongest counter to criticism, especially self-criticism, is through Conversation. It's through healthy conversation with God, and interaction with the Bible, our friends and ourselves, that encouragement and perspective flourish.

1. Allow God to talk to you through the Bible: Philippians 1:6, "Being confident of this, that He who began a good work in you will carry it on to completion until the day of Christ Jesus." That has been a key life verse for me; a verse which reminds me that when things are difficult, or I'm putting myself down, that God isn't done with me yet.

   There are tons of encouragements all throughout the Bible. In the past I have had them printed and stuck to my wall — verses of scripture that encourage me in who I am in Christ Jesus. From time to time, I would look up to that wall and read some of those encouragements out loud to myself. Having those reminders of God's truth spoken over yourself is a really good way to counteract the critical voice in your head.

2. Talk to a Jethro: Another way to counter criticism is to get yourself a Jethro. Jethro was the father-in-law of Moses, and Jethro helped Moses to re-think the way he was leading others. He spotted some flaws in his leadership style and encouraged him to change things, because if he didn't, he was going to burn himself out.

   We all need a Jethro in our lives to talk with. Someone who can come alongside us with experience and encourage us in our leadership, but also point out the areas in our leadership where we need to tweak things to run the race well. I have had several Jethros' influence on my life over the years, and they've been some of my greatest encouragers along the way.

3. We all talk to ourselves, but when you do, be kind to yourself. If you're like me and have that perfectionist streak; if you are hard on yourself and driven, then it can become a recipe for being incredibly self-critical. That's been my experience.

Something I've had to really embrace is the habit of simply being kinder to myself, especially when talking to myself! Often the criticism I will hear, or the thing I will beat myself up over is the stuff that I tell myself in my head. No one else has to say anything, the script will just keep rolling in here. And that can become demoralising. So, we must take control of our thoughts. 2 Corinthians 10:5, 'We take captive every thought to make it obedient to Christ.' As a habit, I've started to say to myself, 'You're doing better than you think!' This is simply to break the cycle of putting myself down.

Whose voice is it that you are listening to? Are you making that thought obedient to Christ? What's the default response you give yourself when you get things wrong or don't measure up to your own expectations? Once you've identified that critical voice in your head you can begin to counter it. And for me, countering it with kindness and through conversation has been a great way to silence it.

And lastly, for countering criticism, alongside consistent conversation with your close friends (rather than isolating yourself) is to get counselling and talk with a counsellor. One of the best things I've done is to get some counselling. The wave of depression I faced over that time is what sparked my need for it and it really was life changing for me personally, but also in my leadership.

There are tons of positives in having counselling, but one of the biggest for me was being able to get perspective. As you'll read in a moment, getting help does not have to be a 'once off' thing. We can ask for help more than once; that's OK. We need to come as we are to this job, but having the self-awareness to realise that God loves us too much to leave us that way is essential if we are to grow in Christlikeness along the way. Try to remain open to getting help consistently. It's proving to be a life saver for me. Having someone help you to unpack your thoughts and get perspective is not to be underestimated, especially if you're an internal processor and get stuck in your own head sometimes.

Sick of Success

If it wasn't clear already, it's worth me saying that these three Cs — comparison, capacity, and criticism, they haven't just disappeared for me. Since discovering these three pitfalls, another key problem that has come up for me is how to deal with the word 'success' when it comes to church planting.

Over the last few months, along with the backlog of the three C's swirling around inside my head which I am trying to bat away daily, the dilemma of 'how to achieve success' in this role has been a cause of great anxiety for me and depression has resurfaced alongside that.

Unfortunately, I think there are many trigger points in this line of work that hack my mental immune system, which I've had to learn to strengthen and build up. For example, the worry, the fear of failure, the constant pressure (99.9% of which is self-inflicted pressure) to attain something that lasts and provides legacy and as a result sickening contemplation and rumination over what the heck 'success' is in this job, has brought me to my knees repeatedly in these early days. I wish I had an 'S' on my chest or that I was one of these heroic leaders you often picture when going on an adventure. However, the reality is that I'm fragile at times and actually, for me, sometimes it's just about being able to get back up again that means one foot can go in front of the other. Sometimes my day is successful simply because I've been able to get out of bed and face the day. I do sometimes ask God, 'Why have you called me into a job that seems to push all my buttons and cause me to struggle in this way?!' And I haven't got an answer really. The only thing I can think of when I ask that is that I am learning to depend on Him more, and that His grace is enough.

For a while I thought I just needed to acclimatise to this new responsibility of leadership, and to a certain extent that is true. I do need to relax into it still, to learn to bear the weight and to adhere to the authority God has given me to lead here. However, what I'm talking about is an unhealthy level of fear and anxiety that has manifested itself.

To give you an idea of how crippling the anxiety has been at times I'll share that recently my wonderful wife booked a surprise overnight getaway for my birthday. At the time of telling me about this, my anxiety was at an all-time high. As a result, I sheepishly asked if we could postpone the trip because of the anxious stress it was causing me in simply thinking about going away for the night. Just let that sink in. I had gotten myself into such an anxious state, that even the thought of going away for a night was causing me incredible stress. The night before we were due to go on this trip, I did not sleep because I was so anxious about simple things such as what to pack in my bag, the potential of traffic and what the room would be like. How ridiculous is that?! I had become completely paralysed due to the build up of anxiety. My wife graciously rearranged the trip and helped me through the process. She is an absolute champion of a woman, and I wouldn't be able to do any of this without her. I thank God for her, but not nearly enough as I should!

Anyway, this climax of anxiety gave me the necessary nudge to face some hard truths about where I have been mentally, emotionally and spiritually over the last few months (and to be honest the last few years). My wife had a stern word for me to get on top of it, otherwise we would have to move on from there, because my mental health had been rapidly declining and she was not prepared for our family to sink because of that – and rightly so. It was time to pick up from where I had left off with my depression and face the inner workings of my behaviour, emotions and thought life.

So, since that evening, I got back into therapy and began carrying out the work needed to get on top of this anxiety and depression and I'm pleased to say that after months of work, prayer, and reflection on this I am doing so much better. But prior struggles I had with mental health aside, where was this present-current anxiety coming from? Putting any past hurts (which we all inevitably have) to one side and focusing on the present: What is it about this job – or rather what it's bringing out in me – that is causing this crippling anxiety? The three main culprits this time around I think have been success, ambition and enjoyment (all of which have become tangled with the three C's along the way).

Here's an attempt to reflect on this and break it down, in the hope that it might help any other first year or emerging church planters get a handle on this quicker than I have.

Some questions to start with:

- How on earth do you know if you are doing well in this line of work?

- What are the criteria for knowing that you are doing a good job as a Priest that plants, or as a Priest at all?

- When does a church plant/graft become successful?

- Is there a magic number that I need for attendance?

- Is success the speed at which you can become sustainable? Is it based on parish share commitments or how many have been through the Alpha course or how many likes we have on our Instagram feed?

To be honest, I'm sick of the word 'success'. It has done me no good whatsoever to plan towards what I think a successful church may look like; no good at all to think how many should be part of our church or even when we feel ready to plant out of our church in the future. Of course I want us to grow, to be healthy in our discipleship, to send out planting teams, to raise up leaders, to see the lost, saved etc. However, at the end of the day, even with all that good stuff happening – does it mean success in God's eyes? The more I dwell on this, the more I wrestle with it and allow it to keep me up at night; the unhealthier I feel about the pursuit of all these good and seemingly fruitful outcomes. I've begun to realise that the metrics used to measure our success, will expose the motive behind our values, and I'm not sure I've liked what I've found hidden in the depths of my motives at times.

Pursuing all these 'successful' things, making these sustainable objectives the focus, has caused me a great deal of stress and anxiety over the last few months, and that's the exact reason why I've made the outcome the focus. I've been allowing what I think the outcomes of a church plant should be to determine my drive. In my 'ambition' to make this thing work, to try and make sure it doesn't fall flat on its face and get struck off as a failure, I have made 'success' an idol and as such, the root for my ambition and enjoyment has become infected, resulting in paralysing anxiety and depression. Our thought life around all this is so important and we must be vigilant with it because the gravity of our action starts with the orbit of our thoughts. So, we need to be mindful of our trajectory. This is why I think it's so important to have people we're accountable to as church planters; people who we know will keep us in check and level-headed.

Over the last couple of years, I have fallen in love with the musical 'Hamilton' – what a show, what a story! I would love to write a sermon series based on the various themes of this show, but to pick one quick theme from it, I would pick the toxic nature of Hamilton's relentless ambition to succeed, the unquenching thirst to make something of himself. Ultimately, it is Hamilton's ambition that causes him to trip over; he is blinded by his quest and as such messes up his work and marriage. During the show, his wife gently confronts him about his ambitious streak and says to him that it would be enough for him to simply stay home with his family rather than work all the hours God has given him; that it would be enough to simply enjoy time at home rather than be elsewhere in his mind working on his ambitious goals to succeed. As I watched this, I couldn't help but sense the Spirit saying to me, 'Paul, if you were to simply sit in the Father's presence, that would be enough; if you were to spend the day in prayer, that would be enough; if you were to be faithful in the little things, that would be enough; if you were to lean back into the Father's embrace and be with Him, that would be enough,' and so on.

Essentially, the outcomes of what a good church plant could look like can go on forever. There's always more that could be done, always more people to reach, to disciple, and so all that stuff will never be enough, because there's always infinitely more to be done. But God isn't calling me to do it all, to have it all together, to be the best church or even the most financially sustainable church; He's simply calling me to be faithful and obedient to Him. That is enough.

This little collection of planting reflections, or rather glorified journal entries, could be the prelude of a book on 'How to Fail as a Church Planter', for all I know (and even if that did end up being the case, then that's great, because at least others can learn from my mistakes). But that's kind of the point. I don't want to write something in ten years' time with rose-tinted glasses that says, 'This is How You Should Do It' or 'Here's a Success Story About a Church Plant'; nor am I so arrogant to assume that any of this will be 'successful'. I want this journaling account to be unfinished and open-ended with the very real possibility that in the world's eyes – the church's eyes even – it could be deemed a complete and utter failure.

I've really wrestled with whether I enjoy this job. So often, it feels so difficult, complicated, messy and just plain uncertain. As such, I'm on a quest now for simplicity in how I lead and lean on God in the process. But perhaps more important than that, I'm on a quest to learn how to simply enjoy God rather than enjoy the job He's given me. Because if I'm honest, and as you will see in the extracts of my 'raw journaling', I have several days where it's clear that I have some very low days in this job and thus not necessarily enjoying it. But I'm learning that that's OK, because ultimately, I'm not called to enjoy my job or to be comfortable in it. My purpose is not to find ultimate satisfaction and joy in my work; it's to find it in my relationship with Jesus.

In his book 'A Long Obedience in the Same Direction', Eugene Peterson writes:

'What is the chief end of man? What is the final purpose? What is the main thing about us? Where are we going, and what will we do when we get there? The answer is, "To glorify God and enjoy Him forever'. Glorify. Enjoy. There are other things involved in Christian discipleship. The Songs of Ascents have shown some of them. But it is extremely important to know the one thing that overrides everything else. The main thing is not work for the Lord; it is not suffering in the name of the Lord; it is not witnessing to the Lord; it is not teaching

Sunday school for the Lord; it is not being responsible for the sake of the Lord in the community, it is not keeping the Ten Commandments; not loving your neighbour; not observing the golden rule. "The chief end of man is to glorify God and enjoy Him forever." Or, in the vocabulary of Psalm 134, "Bless GOD."[13]

This for me, hits the nail on the head when it comes to 'success' and finding contentment in our enjoyment in life with God and the work He calls us to. It's not about the outcomes of the church plant. Yes, I care about those, but I cannot let them define my identity or relationship with the Father, because those things will never be enough. They can never fill the void that they create when they are the main driver for doing what we do. The main driver, the source of our 'ambition', our perseverance must be rooted in our delight in the Lord, to simply glorify Him by being faithful and obedient and to take joy in our relationship with Him. As a result, we are blessed by God, and we get to bless Him in return – maybe that could be our metric for success?

Anxious accomplishment has been my driver for too much of this and, dare I say, a few years of my life. Instead of trying to see myself glorified as a successful church planter and enjoying my job as a result, moving forward I want to live a life determined by seeing God glorified and enjoying Him. I want that to be where I get my perseverance from; not from an

---

[13] Eugene H. Peterson, 'A long obedience in the same direction', p.191-192

expectation of church planters needing to be super ambitious, driven individuals, but from an understanding that my Father in heaven delights in me and that I can take joy in delighting in Him, and as such bless Him in return.

Once again, Eugene Peterson sums this source of our perseverance up far better than me, so I will put the quote below (but do yourself a favour and buy his book – it's brilliant!):

'God sticks to His relationship. He establishes a personal relationship with us and stays with it. The central reality for Christians is the personal, unalterable, persevering commitment God makes to us. Perseverance is not the result of our determination, it is the result of God's faithfulness. We survive in the way of faith not because we have extraordinary stamina but because God is righteous, because God sticks with us. Christian discipleship is a process of paying more and more attention to God's righteousness and less and less attention to our own; finding the meaning of our lives not by probing our moods and motives and morals but by believing in God's will and purposes; making a map of the faithfulness of God, not charting the rise and fall of our enthusiasms. It is out of such a reality that we acquire perseverance.'[14]

---

[14] Eugene H. Peterson, 'A Long Obedience in the Same Direction', p.126

Shadows Prayer

Father, forgive me,
For the times I've compared myself to others,
For the times I've tried to work in someone else's capacity,
For the times I've criticised myself or what You've called me to do.
Help me to minister in the calling You've given me, with the gifts You've equipped me with and with the assurance of Your love for me.

Where my heart has been led astray by anxious ambition,
Steer me back to a place of assured adoration of You,
Help me to live a life that seeks to glorify You and enjoy You;
To do whatever it takes in my being for that to be enough for me,
Help me to desire Your presence and not the outcomes of my labour,
Whatever determination I have, let it be birthed out of Your love and pursuit of me,
Rather than any selfish scheme for worldly success.

In those dark moments – the shadows – shine Your light,
Tilt my head upwards so that I may seek Your face,
release me from the unhealthy burdens I put on myself and give me rest.
Build Your church and help me to glorify and enjoy You in the process,
Amen.

Journaling Point

- What are the stories you're telling yourself?

- Who are you processing your day with?

- Are you receiving counselling, if not, why not?

- How are you measuring success?

- What are you enjoying about your planting role?

- How's your sleep, diet, physical activity?

- What are you doing for fun?

- Are you taking yourself too seriously? Where are you being childlike in your week/conversations/prayers?

PAUL PAVLOU

Chapter 6
Sunrise; Light Overcomes the Darkness

John 1:1-9

'In the beginning was the Word, and the Word was with God, and the Word was God. 2 He was with God in the beginning. 3 Through Him all things were made; without Him nothing was made that has been made. 4 In Him was life, and that life was the light of all mankind. 5 The light shines in the darkness, and the darkness has not overcome it. 6 There was a man sent from God whose name was John. 7 He came as a witness to testify concerning that light, so that through him all might believe. 8 He himself was not the light; he came only as a witness to the light. 9 The true light that gives light to everyone was coming into the world.'

There are good days – lots of them, in fact!

This planting story of ours has certainly been testing over the last year. There is a 'shadow' side to it, which has brought me to my knees at times, and will probably continue to do so at points. Despite the battles – internal and external struggles – my own insecurities being lit up on numerous occasions and the relentless triggering of mental health issues, there are in fact good days; lots of them actually! Even if yesterday is drenched in shadow, and the sun sets with a gloomy feeling, it will rise again in the morning:

Lamentations 3:22–23

[22]'Because of the Lord's great love, we are not consumed, for His compassions never fail.[23] They are new every morning; great is Your faithfulness'.

God has been so good to us throughout this year; I'm sheepishly grateful for the shadow side because it's highlighted God's faithfulness even more. It's forced me to appreciate the sunset and sunrise, to remember that God's got this, that He is the light of the world, and my job is simply to point people to Him.

At the time of writing this, it's still early days for us, so we haven't got some of the big faith testimony stories that you often hear from churches who have been at it a bit longer. And whilst we don't want the fruit of our work to be the only/main source of joy or contentment, I do think we need to celebrate the wins! So, here's a few wins over the last year or so that are worth sharing...

In the last year or so, we've seen:

- People take steps towards Jesus;

- Community beginning to form;

- Team bonding and flourishing in their roles and bringing in others to help serve (and they are an awesome team — each of them an answer to prayer!);

- People making this church their home and someone getting baptised;

- Missional activities taking flight in the community;

- And so many other things along the way too — God has been so good!

All these things add up, and they're rarely on the same day or week, but they are encouraging rays of sunshine and it's important to celebrate them enthusiastically when they happen.

There are two other 'sunrise' moments I'd like to share: The first is when we just moved full time into this planting post, and I was so paranoid about my kids. You know their whole life; their Sunday discipleship has been high quality kids' groups and events with lots of other kids around them and a full-on deal. And I was so worried that moving them into our new context, where there were no groups — only one or two other children, only a traditional service at the time (which our kids aren't mad on) — would affect them negatively. I was so fearful that my kids would hate it and get disillusioned. At the beginning we were at our sending church some weeks and at the plant-graft church other weeks, and on this one particular Sunday, the kids asked me which one we were going to. When I told them that we were going to our sending church, they were both really upset. They were upset we weren't going to the plant-graft church! I couldn't believe it! I thought to myself, why?! Why would you prefer that to all that this other place has to offer? And as I processed it, I think it was down to two things: 1) They had found a sense of belonging at our plant; they felt a unity with me and Hayley in us as a family joining in with this thing and being on an adventure. 2) I think the Holy Spirit had prepared their hearts for this gig long before we arrived and it was such a sunrise moment because it made me realise that God has this under control. I just need to be faithful and obedient.

The other sunrise moment was after one of our earlier services and we had finished tea and coffee, and people that we had inherited from the church we grafted into, were clearing up chairs and tables with the new people that had grafted in with us. It was such a small, simple moment, but it was profound for me, because I'm also praying and stressing about the two pieces of clay forming well together. I remember seeing these two groups of people gelling in this way and I had tears in my eyes because it was the first shoots of unity forming. We've still got a long way to go, but it was enough to give me faith for the next step.

One of the greatest encouragements I have felt so far is the fact that relationships with people are moving from strangers to friendships. Being the introvert I am, I've not always been sure if I'll be able to foster the wide variety of friendships that church life can bring, and which are so crucial of early stages in planting. But God has been gracious in this and I genuinely believe He has softened and grown my heart in this last year. I realised early on in the year, that if I allow myself to get bitter or marinade in frustration, that I will never be able to take things forward in ministry, so I have been simply praying for God to soften and grow my heart for Him – that I would be able to receive more of His love, and as a result be able to love Him more, and then others more too. The irony of this is, that I think it's been the 'shadow' seasons where this growth has formed. It's been the 'proving' time in the shadows that has given space for me to rest and grow in dependence on the Holy Spirit and the friendships I have been making that have helped my heart soften.

Another sunrise moment for me on a personal level rather than a church plant level is when God shared a memory with me that I had forgotten about. I was having a particularly low day – one of those days where it felt like everything was going wrong and I just didn't have a clue what I was doing or how to move forward. On reflection a lot of that 'angst' I was feeling was fear induced: Fear that I wouldn't get things right, or that I would get humiliated and trodden all over. This fear was at its heaviest when I was in an evening prayer space we were running at church, and as I sat there with my head in my hands praying, the Spirit recalled a memory I had long shut away due to the embarrassment it caused me.

The memory was of when I was thirteen years old. I was a pretty chunky thirteen year old, and I often felt a bit shy as a result. One evening I was due to play in a school concert. These were high productions and hundreds of parents would attend. As I got into the car to go to the concert and perform, my trousers split end to end. I can't remember why, but we weren't able to change them, and so I went to this concert with these end-to-end split trousers. You can imagine the fear and anxiety that was building in the car as we drove to the concert. I was a sweaty mess, full of nerves. So, I sat through the concert waiting for my part, and up I got, trousers split, under the spotlight, and I performed my part terribly from start to finish. I felt so humiliated and embarrassed, and I just wanted to go home and forget the whole thing.

As I sat there in church reliving this unfortunate memory, I said to God, 'Why are you showing me this again? I had hoped to never remember it!' To which the Spirit replied, 'You got up and played your part regardless of the fear and humiliation. You could have stayed home and avoided it, but you chose to go to the concert and play even though you knew it would be an unpleasant experience – you did it anyway. And that is why you are the one I have called here to do what you are doing. You knew it would be hard, but you came to do it anyway. And I'm right here with you. So even if you get humiliated, even if you get scared and even if you're a sweaty mess wanting to hide, I know you're going to get up and do it anyway because that's who I've created you to be." With tears in my eyes as I felt the Spirit encouraging me with this, I felt a huge sense of relief, relief in knowing that it's OK if I feel a bit of fear from time to time, or even a bit embarrassed, because at the end of the day, He's wired me to do what I'm doing regardless. That gave me the confidence to stop hiding my light under a bowl, because if I'm honest, I found myself doing this, allowing fear to creep in and cover up my light. In fact, I felt so convicted of this that I repented to my team about it in one of our team meetings, about the fact that I wasn't always leading from a place of being who God has called me to be in this place, due to the fear taking over at times.

Hearing the Spirit whisper this memory back through His view of it changed the narrative for me. For all these years I've seen that memory as a humiliating negative, but God saw it as a strength; He saw in me what I couldn't. In that moment, He convicted me to lead as me, Paul, not as anyone else or to please anyone else, but simply as me. And yes, I will get things wrong; I will probably embarrass myself on numerous occasions, but I know from previous experience, that with Jesus' help I will do the job anyway. My father-in-law said to me once, 'Nothing is wasted.' This memory experience really showed me that. So, if there is pain in your memory, if there is shadow in your past, maybe allow God to play it to you through His lens and see what He's saying to you through it — it might just help you face the current battle you're in!

Whilst I wouldn't wish hardships on any emerging church planters out there, I would say that you should expect it, and find a way to grow through the challenge when it comes. For weeks I questioned my competency when things felt tough, I thought I was simply doing it all wrong because it felt difficult, or I kept hitting barriers. And I did make mistakes, for sure, but I also think that in our job description we should have something that says, 'It's OK if this is difficult! It may not be what you thought, and that's OK!'

Sunrise and shadow are two sides of the same coin, and too often, I have allowed myself to think that the two can't co-exist; that because it's hard I'm simply not called to it and that I should just give up. But even as I write this, I can recall breakthroughs that have happened just this week that I would never have seen coming even a month ago. Each week I catch myself thinking, Well that's not gone the way I thought it would! But you know what, that's OK! I'm still here. Tomorrow will come regardless, and Jesus is going to build His church; so chill out and keep looking up. The sun's still shining. You're doing great!

Sunrise Prayer

Jesus, I don't want to pray for people reading this today to be super church planters,
I want to pray for them, for myself,
to be more captivated by You,
by Your heart for us.

I pray for a church of captivated disciples,
A church that knows just how much You are captivated by us,
God, I thank You that we move Your heart,
There's nothing we can do to earn it,
We can't pave the way to Your heart with our own achievements,
but through Jesus we can be with You,

with Jesus we can become more like You.

Bless us with a praise-filled perspective,
That looks to You and trusts in Your goodness,
Being confident that Your light overcomes the darkness.

Help us to be captivated by Your presence more and more each day,
Help our hearts to soften,
To have hearts captivated by Your heart for us,
Amidst all the distractions.
Help us to have the discipline to sit at Your feet in awe-struck wonder,
Allowing our discipleship to move from head to heart,
And become more like You,
Amen.

Action

Alongside your daily devotional, carve out two hours of your day off to 'dwell' in God's presence. Be it through books, worship, a long walk, silence, whatever – just make sure you have that time spent, and don't beat yourself up with trying to cram everything in. Just get the week off your chest and surrender it to God. Then allow the Holy Spirit to minister to you and give yourself a pat on the back whilst you're at it – you're doing better than you think!

PAUL PAVLOU

Chapter 7:
Snippets; Raw Diary Entries

This journal started from my initial attempts to process and then write raw entries as I tried to reflect and work out what on earth was going on. I've added a few of them here for you to read.

20 August 2021, 9:41pm
Battle of Mind

Have been aware of my thought life this week. It's nothing new for me to wrestle with, but it's been a bit of a battle this week fending off negative thoughts about myself as a leader and of ministry going forward. Doing OK, but it's just a bit tiring sometimes pushing back at that stuff.

21 August 2021, 11:31am
Move Day!

Currently sat in the car in the service station waiting for Hayley and the kids to finish from the loo. We left our house and are heading to drop off a few bits (the Lego) at our new place, then we will go to a hotel for a night and then an AirBnB.

So far the kids have handled it well and Hayley and I are fine. Feeling a bit tired as expected but glad to be out of the old house and venturing to the new. Really ready to move on now – excited about the new chapter with its challenges and prospects alike. Help me Lord, to enjoy all of it and keep a healthy perspective throughout!!

22 August 2021, 9:18am
What If?!

It's partly down to the stress of the move but I have been really tense and anxious over the last forty-eight hours. All sorts of 'what if' questions and doubts over my new role bombarding my thoughts, i.e. What if they don't get on board with the changes I make? What if I'm no good at it? What if the whole thing is a nightmare? What if I don't get on with the wardens? What if I'm horrible at change management? What if they're all against me?! What if I can't manage all the different strands to the role?! What if it's all too much?! What if I feel trapped and claustrophobic in the role? What if?! What if?! What if?!

Had to get a hold of myself and find the thought behind the thought. Find the evidence. Obviously, there's no evidence for these negative questions: they're lies and fear induced.

Take your time.
Build the scaffold.
Invest in relationships.
You're not alone.
Enjoy the process.
Keep perspective.
God's got you.

22 August 2021, 6:44pm
From AirBnB Bedroom Window

Sat down for a moment in an AirBnB bed whilst waiting to get kids to bed and just began to think about the future and then this rainbow appeared. Just felt like a little nod from God saying, 'Don't worry, I've got you'...

29 August 2021, 4:42pm
So We've Moved to Coventry!

We moved about four days ago and it's been non stop since – unpacking and sorting the house. Haven't had time to pray or get into any of my normal routines etc. which has been tiring. But we're here and getting things sorted in time for me to start working and kids go to school. Weirdest thing about my work is that now that we've landed here, I feel like I've forgotten everything; like I've never worked in a church or thought about church planting. It feels like somebody has just wiped that area of my brain! Maybe that's a good thing and I can see things with a clear view. Must admit I am feeling pretty overwhelmed already at the magnitude of what needs to be done and the anticipation of having potentially tricky conversations in my mind, but I just need to keep getting perspective and remember that at the end of the day, the Spirit is going to do what He wants and I just need to take it one day at a time and not give in to the pride of thinking it's all on me and I have to sort everything asap.

Hayley has been feeling a bit shell shocked, I think. It's hard for her. She's doing well though. The kids are happy and coping well with the change – it's new schools for them next week!

Lord Jesus, please help me manage this new role and to start things off in the right way with work-life balance, learning my environment and seeking Your will for each bit, as there's so many different options for how to do it all and when etc. Also feel quite nervous about the St Mark's work I'll be doing in my first term – lots of new stuff. Need to keep remembering that my experience + God's Spirit is enough for me to get through it all. And hey – even if I mess up, is it really that bad??? No, of course it isn't! Even if I mess the whole job up entirely and we leave here without achieving anything – what does it really matter? What matters is that we've been obedient and at least tried. Jesus, help me to be obedient to you everyday in everything, please Lord. I really need to know Your presence.

Need my routines to be established asap as they really help me get grounded and centred on God. Please help with that too Jesus – oh, and my meeting with all the wardens next week and the licensing, the service I'm covering on 12 September and St Mark's stuff too!! It's weird, I feel like I've forgotten how to preach too!! Oh Jesus, help me!

30 August 2021, 9:15am
First Trip to the Local Pub in Wyken!

Like the local pub – cheap, close with decent food (I may have chipped my tooth eating a burger... That'll teach me to use a fork!).

15 September 2021, 9:36pm
It's Been Busy

It's been a busy few days, trying to sort stuff at St Ms and get meetings booked in with Wyken churches etc.

Favourite bit so far is walking with Reggie and stopping to talk to the locals. Have met so many people already and got to know their names and chat. Feels like it's all part of the 'scaffolding' side of things. Need to be patient and remember I'm only two weeks into the role! Wearing a dog collar has been good around the locals and engaging in conversations. Feeling tired and just wanting to make sure I'm getting the right balance of St Ms and Wyken stuff in, without getting distracted by unnecessary tasks.

18 September 2021, 8:16am
Horrible Dream

Had a horrible dream last night that a woman jumped at me and was strangling me. I could tell straight away she wasn't really a woman, but was in fact a demon. As I was being strangled the face changed into a horrible demonic one and was just laughing and shouting at me and I was trying to pray out, but it was strangling me and I was struggling to get my voice out and find the words to say. Anyway, the dream woke me up and then I couldn't sleep for two hours or so, due to stressing about the plant and not having 'vision' yet or when to get staff or that people don't know us enough to come with us, etc. Ah, the joys of planting!

20 September 2021, 9:47pm
Pendulum!

Well, I feel like I'm on an ongoing pendulum of being overwhelmed by everything that needs to be done and in the same breath knowing God is in control of it all!

It's like I'm playing table tennis with myself and running around the table to keep returning the ball. Feel a bit stressed by all the meetings I've got and not enough time for things like sermon prep and spending time around Wyken.

21 September 2021, 10:00am
God Scaffolding Me

Realising that as I'm trying to build scaffolding in relationships with others, that God is putting scaffolding around me to prep me.

27 September 2021
Walk with Kim and Lisa[15]

Was looking for nature area to walk Reggie and bumped into Kim* from the parish who ended up showing me where it was and walking me around. Then we bumped into a neighbour who is also a Christian and she walked me home! Was lovely to spend time with them and get to know them a bit. Especially as I feel constantly guilty about not being with these people in both churches more. Felt like God was just sending me people I needed to see and connect with. Thank you God – more please!

7 October 2021, 10:47pm
Got To Get Up

Feeling better today following that difficult meeting. Realised it's really not the end of the world. This is part of the job; that disappointments and not meeting people's expectations are part of the job; that God will deal with it; that I will have to roll with the punches; that I have to stay true to who I am and what I feel called too. I can't allow unresolved problems, people or situations to keep me under because I simply won't last if that happens. Whatever comes of it, I will deal with and will trust that God will provide and do His thing. Who knows what will happen, but God's going to sort it out either way, isn't He! I'm not here to please people or do their bidding.

---

[15] Not real names.

I'm just here to be faithful and obedient to God. Get up!

9 October 2021, 10:14pm
Revitalisation Realisation

Realised this week that the problems I encounter should be an encouragement with regard to church and ministry, because I'm here to revitalise. It's because of how I'm made, because of my skill set and gifts, that I'm placed here to serve in this capacity. So with that it has given me a perspective where problems are part of it and I'm here to bring about solutions with the help of the Spirit and God's people. That puts me on a much more positive footing than being disheartened every time an issue occurs. Thank You, God. Help me to continue to get better at that and solve problems well and with a good outlook and reliance on You.

15 November 2021, 8:06am
Feeling Low and Lost

Realised I have been feeling really quite low lately. I feel so out of control, like I'm just hovering from one church to the next without really being able to thrive in any of them and constantly out of my comfort zone. Wrestling with anxiety and depression is not a new phenomenon; it's just frustrating that they're rearing their head so early on in my time here in Coventry. If I feel like this so early on, does that mean

I won't last in this role? Have I pursued this role for the wrong reasons and misheard God? Am I not designed for this job? Would I be better suited to something with less stress points on change/success/failure? Maybe I'm not suited to leading others? Perhaps I'm better as someone who follows orders, does the job and lets someone else handle the overall responsibility? Another misplaced leader statistic? Could really do with a significant win at the moment. Just feels like a slow slog everyday at the moment and this is just the beginning.

15 November 2021, 8:21am
Poor Hayley

Feel bad for Hayley at the moment. I'm not much fun to be around. I know I've turned within myself and irritable to others. She's bearing the brunt of that. Someone commented the other day saying that I was such a 'gentle' character. Gosh, I wish that were so. Most of the time in my head I'm screaming all sorts of things whilst trying to remain calm on the outside with those around me or who I'm trying to disciple. Does that mean I'm being fake? Or is it good to have restraint? Maybe I should speak my mind more? Although in the past, where I've allowed myself to be my inner blunt self, it hasn't always gone that well – perhaps there's a middle ground? I wonder if this was the case for all those others I've looked on in the past who are or at least seem incredibly gentle and calm. I wonder if they too were going back home and punching the punch bag from the sheer overwhelming nature of this work. Probably not — I imagine that's just me.

16 November 2021, 4:59am
Insomnia

Ah, insomnia, my old friend. It seems you've come to visit again. Have been up since just before 3am (it's now 5am) and will remain awake now. Over the last two to three hours, I've managed to spend my night thinking about church finances, my preach this coming Sunday, student work, my podcast, the need for church planting to become normal in the CofE, various ideas of how to revitalise two churches at once, the Christmas bazaar this Saturday (from which I have no idea what to expect), the prayer meeting I'm leading in the morning and a bunch of conversations I need to have.

I've never been a good sleeper and it's not been great over the last month. It's partly, well mostly, stress-related I think and probably because I've felt low over the last couple of weeks. It feels like I've been having to fight harder recently against depression and anxiety; both have felt more apparent than usual, and the air has been thicker as a result. I think for whatever reason, both are worse this time of year for me.

Everything feels like a slog at the moment and the insomnia isn't helping. Help please, God.

20 November 2021, 12:31pm
Christmas Bazaar

Had a great time at the bazaar today. Met and spoke with lots of the locals in the area – the place was absolutely packed. Felt like a great day of connecting with others. I'm blown away by the hard work of the folk at church; they have worked their socks off today, so servant-hearted! I also had a conversation with a potential curate who I think would be amazing! Praying she feels the same way about the opportunity to come and work with me and the plant – come on Lord, please!!!!

24 November 2021, 7:58am
Are You Enjoying It?

To a certain extent enjoying the 'fruit' of the work is natural and OK, but I wonder if I'm setting myself up for a huge fall if I'm only finding joy in the labour from the fruit that comes from it? What if I never get to see the fruit of the work? What if the fruit is being saved for someone else to reap? Will I love a life of hard work and graft without enjoying that which I've been called into? I sincerely hope not – so then how? How do I get to a place of enjoying that which I am presently engaging with, without relying on the potential fruit of it to see me through?

29 November 2021, 9:03pm
Church planting is like choosing to walk on an uphill, icy road.

Was walking the dog earlier and the pavement I was walking on was ridden with ice and hard to walk on without falling over. I looked over the road to see that the parallel pavement on the opposite side of the road had no ice at all! And yet, I deliberately chose to stay on the icy pavement. Even though each step risked me slipping over getting hurt; even though it took twice as long and even though there was an easier option just a couple of metres away, I chose to walk this icy path. And therein lies the path of a church planter – be it stupidity or sheer stubbornness to see something through. That spoke to me today about why God has called me to this niche of church ministry. Thankfully, I didn't slip and fall, but it took bloomin' ages to get home!

10 March 2022, 11:21am
'Paul, you're a vicar. Why don't you do anything for me?'

Took the dog over to chat with Daniella.[16] Not going to do all the things that I'm asked to do by others, but I can go and spend time with them for a simple conversation. Sometimes that's all it is.

---

[16] Not real name.

11 March 2022, 2:20pm

I'm beginning to think that to live as a church planter is to live a life of inconvenience.

14 March 2022, 9:57pm

Been in this job about six months, and I've decided that plans are overrated.

27 March 2022, 4:40pm
Praying Our Worry

The last few days I've been worrying about finding cover for Sunday services when I'm not around (I don't have a team yet, so it's just me), and only this morning would you believe, did I think to pray. I haven't found cover yet but feel far less worried because at least now, I've given it to God.

Why does it always take me so long to bring things to my Heavenly Father? I think it's because I am in the habit of underestimating His goodness and care. Sorry Father. Help me to rest in Your embrace more readily!

8 April 2022, 7:05am
Success?

I've been thinking a lot lately about what success looks like and I need to dwell on it a lot more still. But out of that thinking and off the back of another church leader's advise on success being framed by what state my marriage is in by the end of my ministry, I am wondering if these three hopes for my future could possibly be some sort of target for my future as an older man in the big three areas of my life (faith, family/friends, work/ministry).

Faith: That I am still in relationship with Jesus and have fallen immeasurably more in love with Him as a result.

Family/friends: That I am still married to my wonderful wife and have a flourishing/thriving marriage in my old age. In a good, strong relationship with my gorgeous children, along with a solid group of healthy friendships that have grown and matured over the years.

Work/ministry: That I can make it to one day be that old boy in church (still full of love and passion for the church and its kingdom work) that cheers on the church leader and their team, letting them know that they're doing a great job.

24 March 2022, 1:35pm
CBT Workbook Exercise Notes on Core Fears

Fears: You'll be alone. You're a bad leader. You're a failure.

28 February 2022
Vision and Prayer Night

Wow! What an encouragement tonight was!

We had a bunch of people from St Mark's along with a handful from the existing church community. It was SO good to worship with everyone together. We worshipped, shared some of the vision and prayed together. There was a real buzz around the room and it was such fun.

Probably the best bit about it was leading the evening with Hayley. I struggled to hold back the tears as she opened the Vision talk part – just standing back watching her lead was so moving and it reminded me of the privilege that it is doing this job with her; in fact, I couldn't do it without her!

Someone from the existing congregation hugged us at the end of the night, saying that they have been praying for this for years and now it feels like it might be happening, i.e. a new season starting for the church and the community – may it be so, Lord!

8 March 2022, 4:42pm
Home Group

Had the loveliest time with a home group from the church we're grafting into today. It was so good to spend time with them as they unpacked God's word, worshipped and prayed. Really encouraging and such a joy to spend time with people in this way!

13 March 2022, 2:10pm
A Moment Together

We haven't fully grafted into the existing church congregation yet but today a couple of families who are exploring to join us at the Plant came along. After the service there was a small but significant moment where someone from the existing congregation asked for help to put the chairs and tables away. As I began to put things away, I glanced up to see the existing congregation and those joining us (along with their children) all packing tables and chairs away together. It was one of those moments where I felt prompted just to hold my gaze and witness the joining together of two families becoming one. It was such a small thing but impacted me massively and warmed my heart to see family being forged through the simple act of packing chairs away!

Thank You, Jesus!

16 March 2022, 8:20am
Man Telling Me to Quit in Dream

Last night I dreamt there was a large, angry man shouting at me saying, "Just quit! You're not going to be any good as a church leader! Just take this (some random gift) and be on your way!" And in the dream, I could see myself getting deflated, but there was a presence there speaking to me saying, "You've got this. You can do it. You're doing great!" Then I took the gift and threw it in the large man's face and told him to get lost.

Then in the dream I began praying. I prayed for a bigger heart, acknowledging that my heart isn't big and soft enough for this; that I need to love God more, to love myself more (in a healthy way) and to love others more. Then I began praying for God to break my heart more for the lost and the church and was in tears doing so.

Then I woke up struggling to breathe, with a banging headache because I'm currently down with COVID.

30 March 2022, 10:06pm
Amazing What Encourages You

I was chatting with some of the existing congregation of the church we are grafting into this evening. During the conversation I mentioned how I've started driving to the area where the church building is situated, in order to take the dog for a walk around there and to prayer walk the patch with him. After I'd shared this, one of the lovely ladies commented on how all the Vicars here over the years have walked their dogs around the area that I mentioned. I know it's probably ridiculous, but just hearing that I've been joining in with the prayer walking in that place and in the same manner (with the dog by my side) just really encouraged me. It encouraged me that maybe I'm doing something right – even if it's as simple as just prayer walking with the dog in the right place. That'll do.

2 April 2022, 5:33pm
Anxious Head < Adoring Heart

Have had a few difficult days lately where the anxiety is kicking about and leaving me weary; anxiety over those under my care and how they are and if I'm handling things correctly and all the obsessive compulsive 'what if' questions that come with that. When I finally try to take a breath and hit the stop button with all these thoughts and actually bring it to Jesus, I find Him giving me a very simple answer: 'compassion.' 'Allow compassion for the church to flood your heart. Ask Me for a bigger and softer heart; a heart shaped and cared for by Me and a heart that rests in the rhythm of My own heart for you.'

And then it all seems so simple. All the anxieties over this church planting, all the anxieties over the change management taking place and the tricky conversations and the anticipated conflict of doing things differently, suddenly feels lighter.

The situation hasn't changed, nor the things that I get anxious about, but just having the reassuring simplicity from God that all I need to do is receive His love and in turn love Him and those in my life, brings a freedom. I suddenly don't feel like I'm responsible for the outcome of an impending matter or a person's reaction, but instead focused on my heart's posture towards them and the scenario. I suddenly don't feel myself building up premeditated defences to disagreement, but a vulnerability to receive them and try my best to offer a loving response in return — to ask for help rather than to ask for respect.

8 April 2022, 7:15pm
Review the Week

The week's not over yet. Still two more days left, but I thought it worth a review to reflect on the positives. There have certainly been some difficulties and tricky moments, some of which have really hurt. Nonetheless, there's been some beautiful moments too. Such as:

- On Sunday someone from the existing congregation said they could see what I was trying to do going forward with the church, when I shared some of the vision. They were excited by it! So encouraging!

- Somebody said they were interested in joining the plant team.

- Spending time with other planters on a zoom call and encouraging one another.

- Spending time at a local school as part of an Easter event.

- Spending time with the lovely people at afternoon tea at church and having a laugh with them.

- •Chewing the fat over the Holy Spirit and evangelism with people on our lent course.

- Having a Zoom call with my prayer quad putting the world to rights.

- Going out for lunch with a friend from church and getting to know each other some more.

- Treated to an amazing lunch by my dad for my birthday.

It's so easy to get bogged down in things I find difficult and to let that rob me of the joyous moments Jesus has blessed me with. I've got to work harder at keeping things in perspective and not being so hard on myself. I fear I'll miss out on the joys of life that are right in front of me if I do. Still two more days to go!!!! Who knows what other blessings God will bring!

Help me to get perspective, Lord, and to see the work You're doing right in front of me, Holy Spirit. Give me the wisdom and grace to focus and reflect on the good moments rather than being blinded by the battles.

26 April 2022, 6:41am
Our First Signing!

Last night we received a text from an amazing couple to say that they would like to join the church plant! This was so unexpected, and we are absolutely thrilled that they want to join in with the story here! Thank You, Jesus!

26 April 2022, 9:40pm
More Sign Ups!

We've just had another two couples say they want to join us this evening! This is mental! Literally have no words! This whole thing is one mad rollercoaster!

26 April 2022, 10:27pm
Hat Trick

Well, we've got a third! Just speechless really. God is so good and these people are just amazing. I'm in total awe of them for even considering it. Just wow!

30 April 2022, 7:08pm
First Sunday Full Time!

Well tomorrow is our first Sunday officially full time at the church we're grafting into. It will be the normal traditional service that we're joining in with (not starting the new one till later in the year), but there'll potentially be people there who are joining us from our sending church, as well as all the faithful existing congregation. The existing congregation has been so patient with me and this phasing-in approach to the church. It's not been easy for them, but they have been very gracious to us.

I feel all sorts of things tonight in anticipation for tomorrow. It's been such a lot of work just to get to this milestone and I'm very aware of how much more work is about to come my way too.

Feel excited, tired, nervous, but also at peace that we get to be all in in this church and the community now. Not sure how much sleep I'll get tonight. I just really want the two congregations to unite cohesively into a real family. I think we are on the precipice of a season of 'holy chaos' over the next six to nine months (at least).

I wish I could get a glimpse into the future in five years' time to see that everything is OK, or at least if it isn't, that we're content in God, nonetheless!

Come on, Jesus – come and do Your thing tomorrow... please?!

1 May 2022, 8:35am
Nightmare Dream Ahead of First Full Time Service

Well, low and behold I slept terribly last night ahead of today's Sunday gathering. When I did manage to sleep, I had a nightmare about what must have been the world's worst church Sunday Service. Everything that could have gone wrong in this service went wrong; absolutely everything! Woke up in a nervous sweat, praying that this would not be the case today or ever!

Anyway, the kids came into our bed when they woke up as they usually do and I shared my 'nightmare', to which they replied, 'That doesn't sound like a nightmare – that sounds funny.' Pausing and pondering on this for a few seconds, I replied, 'Yeah, I suppose it does really.' And just like that, the fear over the service/church plant going horribly wrong dissipated – through the simple remark of a child.

And maybe that's the thing: I need to work on my perspective and become more childlike in how I think through this stuff perhaps, with the knowledge of God as my Father who has it under control!

Well, here we go then – off to church!!

1 May 2022, 5:04pm
It Went OK!

Our first full time Sunday at the church and it wasn't a nightmare! In fact, it was pretty fun. We had some folk from our sending church begin to join in and it was so lovely to see some children in church. The cherry on top was that another family has committed to joining the church plant – once again, I'm amazed by the faith of these people and their willingness to join in. Thank You, God.

8 May 2022, 1:03pm
People Coming Together

I had to shoot off from church today to go to a meeting, so I wasn't going to be around to help build connections between people who are joining us from the sending church and the existing congregation. So, I was worried people wouldn't chat or spend time with each other. But I've clearly underestimated people as lots did stay with the existing congregation to chat and spend time with them to build relationship. I was so encouraged by this and it has moved me incredibly to see both groups of people coming together in this way. All such amazing people!

9 May 2022, 5:51pm
Mother Smiling at Baby

Just sat in the train, looking out the window, and noticed a mother pushing a buggy and giving the biggest grin of glee to her baby as she was walking. A beautiful expression to witness, grateful to have spotted such a tender moment in time – puts things into perspective!

24 May 2022, 7:46am
Church Plant Birth

Just realised that we have been sent out from our sending church to graft into the existing church we're planting into, having been there for nine months. It's like this time has been the pregnancy and now we're amid labour-birth. I think there's something quite special in the timing!

9 June 2022, 10:06pm

PCC went really well tonight – so pleased!

12 July 2022
Sports Days

I was so proud of Evangeline and Zachary and learnt so much from them in their sports days. In Zachary's egg and spoon race, he walked so painfully slow to try and keep the egg on the spoon, and he kept dropping the egg, with all the other kids zooming by and finishing way ahead of him. But he was undeterred; the whole way he kept looking up at me to check in, then down at the egg, then up at me again. Never did he look to see where the other kids were in the race. He just kept focused on what he had to do and as he did, so he kept looking up at me, all the way to the end. He finished last and didn't even care because he had finished what he set out to do. All that mattered to him was that he finished and that his dad was with him throughout it. I have so much to learn from him; not to worry about what other church planters are doing or how well they are doing; not to compare my race to theirs; not to look up at other spectators and seek their approval or recognition, but rather to keep looking up to God, knowing that He is cheering me and the church on every slow step of the way. In one of Evangeline's races, she was on her way to coming last, but as she was realising this in the race, her face got a determined look and she really pushed herself, overtaking her friend just before the finish line. I'm not bothered about whether she would have been last or not, what I loved was her determination to not give up and to push herself through it. She persevered and dug deep when she could have just taken her foot off the gas. And she celebrated graciously too, which I loved. Even when we got home, she wasn't going on about it, which was really lovely. Lots to learn from her in this.

13 July 2022, 9:23am
Painfully Aware

Woke up earlier today feeling painfully aware of mistakes I may be making. Feel like I've made so many in the space of just a few months. Also, I am aware of people I've known over the years who have left churches because they've been hurt by someone in leadership (granted those incidents haven't always been the leaders' fault). No one likes to see that happen. I suppose I just don't want my silly mistakes along the way to derail anyone from their walk with Jesus. I don't think that's been the case so far but has been weighing on me since waking up. So many of the things I find myself concerned with, are not things I thought I'd be fretting over. So much of this isn't what I thought it would be, and quite often I've been surprised at how I react to things and the ways it's made me question how and why we 'do' church and leadership the way we do and how we raise up others in the process.

Conclusion: Summing up; I Don't Know How This Will All Pan Out, And That's OK!

This glorified diary of the run up to my first year in planting and the initial few months of it is finishing inconclusive. I have purposefully stopped writing at this point because this isn't meant to be a success or failure story. It is simply a recording of observations and reflections made along the way and is far from complete. There remain many shadows and sunrise moments that I have left out. The truth is, that no matter how much we plan, write, strategize and so forth, at the end of the day, God is going to do what He wants to do. We in response, are to learn contentment in how it all looks in His eyes – especially in the 'shadow' moments. So, rather than try to round this off as a finished product (which it deliberately isn't), I am leaving it open-ended.

I don't know what God will do – whether it will grow, or whether it will flop. I just want to do what my dad has always told me to do, which is to be faithful and know that the God who has called me is faithful and He will do it!

In many ways, it's not what I thought it would be. It probably won't be what I think. Both of these are OK. These last few write ups of my journey in its earliest stages have really been me simply unpacking the inner process of learning to be content in Christ; content with the present calling God has given me and working out how to lead through it to the best of my ability. I also choose to be content in knowing that God has me when I wake up feeling fearful of the day ahead and will be walking alongside me through it all. I choose to be content in trusting that Jesus will build His church.

As mentioned in the introduction, a key take away or strap-line I've taken away from this process, and would offer to others is, to do the prep, go gently and embrace the small wins along the way. It's been a humbling eye-opener to the truth of my fragilities, weaknesses, insecurities and brokenness, only to reveal that God still loves me and has called me nonetheless to this work. More importantly, He calls me His own, His child. It's also been incredibly encouraging and faith-building to see the Spirit at work in this place, and to be able to live this life with Hayley, Evangeline, Zachary and a truly amazing team.

There is much to be thankful for and I'm grateful to have had the opportunity to give it a go. It's my prayer that this book will encourage; that it would encourage emerging leaders, especially budding church planters, as they discern, prepare for and head into their first year of planting. It's my prayer that this book will also equip them with hope as they travail their own highs and lows!

Wrap Up and Prayer

Within the time span of writing this, there have been many cycles and patterns of ups and downs. A weekly cycle that often kicks up all these emotions and experiences, somehow managing to encapsulate them week by week, is of course our Sunday gatherings! Sunday keeps coming around, and it keeps testing and hitting insecurities, ego, nerves, whilst simultaneously being able to bring huge encouragement and amazing encounters.

As the Sunday gathering seems to capture so much of what I've experienced throughout this journal, I thought it would be good to end the whole thing with a prayer I have written to pray and use for myself at the end of a Sunday gathering, to help me process the whole thing and give it back to God:

Post Gathering Prayer

Father,
Another gathering has finished,
Another Sunday served.
Thankful for Your grace to get through it,
Far more than I deserve.

My head and heart are full
of conversation, concern and creativity.
Help me in this moment,
In this post gathering lull,
To be still and to hold every thought captive,

And not let it trigger me.

Help me to let all that I need to let go of
Drift – away...
Only leaving the whisper of encouragement,
To resonate the rest of the day.

Help me Spirit,
Not to be burdened by that which was hard,
Nor to run away with scenarios that are out of my control.
Help me to delight in all that was hopeful,
To lay down all that was hurtful.

Where there was disappointment;
Help me to accept that I am loved by You,
Regardless of what was said or left unachieved.
To not fret of how I was perceived or if others were aggrieved;
But solely remember that You are the One I aim to see pleased.

Jesus,
There is so much I long to see when we gather,
Such potential for growth and breakthrough!
At times such rejoicing at what is happening here and now,
But still so much to sow and plough!

Help me, Jesus,
To remember that it's You who builds the church;
To remember to get a grip either when I just don't know how this will work or

When it all seems to be going brilliantly and can't be contained;
To remember that Sunday will come again with a new set of highs and lows;
To remember that You've got this,
That it's Your church,
No matter how my preaching goes.

Help me
In this weird moment,
This paradoxical post gathering
Lament and laughter –
To entrust my service and those serving to You,
Here and ever after.

Help me, Jesus,
To shepherd from a place of knowing,
That I too go astray,
That I too drifted from the ninety-nine,
That I too was sought after by You.
May I never grow so disheartened that I stop pursuing the lost,
May I never allow my heart to harden and Pharaoh the flock, but rather
May I flock towards them in haste as I tread,
With arms wide open,
Reckless in how I lavishly love instead.

Turn my complaint into compassion,
My fear into courage,
My insecurity into assurance
That You'll get me through, and

My grievance into gratitude,
So that I'm ready for next Sunday,
When I get to ride this rollercoaster all over again with You!
Amen.

About the Author

Paul Pavlou leads a church plant-graft in Coventry with his wife Hayley, children (Evangeline & Zachary) and Reggie – the dog. He is also the creator and host of the 'Church Plant Chat' podcast which is designed to equip emerging church planters with learnings from UK based Church Planters. Paul is passionate about wanting to encourage, equip and empower others – especially in the world of Church Planting!

'Journal of a Church Planter' Video Series

Paul Pavlou, Vicar of St Mary Magdalene with Risen Christ, in Wyken, Coventry, unpacks his journals of planting a church in this seven-part video series. Joined in conversation by Helen Shannon, Estates Ministry lead of CCX, each episode sees Paul explore the everyday realities of following God's call, the challenges and joys of grafting, and what God has taught him along the way. It is the ideal starting point for anyone wanting to hear first-hand experiences of what answering God's invitation to plant can entail.

Each episode is linked to each chapter of the book – why not finish each chapter with its matching episode?

Video Series link:

'Church Plant Chat' Podcast

A podcast hearing from UK based Church Planters about their leadership experiences. It is designed to equip and encourage both emerging and current Church Planters/Leaders. It can be found on Spotify and most other streaming platforms.

PAUL PAVLOU

About PublishU

PublishU is transforming the world of publishing.

PublishU has developed a new and unique approach to publishing books, offering a three-step guided journey to becoming a globally published author!

We enable hundreds of people a year to write their book within 100-days, publish their book in 100-days and launch their book over 100-days to impact tens of thousands of people worldwide.

The journey is transformative, one author said,

"I never thought I would be able to write a book, let alone in 100 days... now I'm asking myself what else have I told myself that can't be done that actually can?"

To find out more visit
www.PublishU.com

PAUL PAVLOU

Printed in Great Britain
by Amazon

41379628R00086